SO-AAC-406

Best Hikes With
CHILDREN®
in Western Washington

Best Hikes With CHILDREN®
in Western Washington

VOLUME 1

SECOND EDITION

By Joan Burton
Photos by Bob & Ira Spring

THE
MOUNTAINEERS

Published by
The Mountaineers
1001 SW Klickitat Way, Suite 201
Seattle, WA 98134

© 1998 text by Joan Burton, photos by Bob and Ira Spring

All rights reserved

Second edition, 1998

No part of this book may be reproduced in any form, or by any electronic, mechanical, or other means, without permission in writing from the publisher.

Published simultaneously in Great Britain by Cordee, 3a DeMontfort Street, Leicester, England, LE1 7HD

Manufactured in the United States of America

Edited by Julie Hall
Maps by Gray Mouse Graphics
Photographs by Bob and Ira Spring
Cover design by Watson Graphics
Book design by Bridget Culligan
Layout by Gray Mouse Graphics
Cover photograph: *Family campsite in the Tatoosh Range of Mount Rainier National Park* ©Kirkendall/Spring

Library of Congress Cataloging-in-Publication Data
Burton, Joan, 1935–
    Best hikes with children in western Washington/by Joan Burton; photos by Bob & Ira Spring.—2nd ed.
        p.   cm.
    Rev. ed. of: Best hikes with children in western Washington & the Cascades. c1988–c1992
    Includes index.
    ISBN 0-89886-564-6 (v. 1)
    1. Cascade Range—Guidebooks. 2. Northwest, Pacific—Guidebooks. 3. Hiking—Washington (State)—Guidebooks. 4. Mountaineering—Cascade Range—Guidebooks. 5. Family recreation—Northwest, Pacific—Guidebooks. 6. Children—Travel—Northwest, Pacific—Guidebooks. 7. Washington (State)—Guidebooks. 8. Cascade Range—Guidebooks. 9. Northwest, Padivid—Guidebooks. I. Burton, Joan, 1935–   Best hikes with children in western Washington & the Cascades. II. Title.
GV199.42.W2B87   1998
917.97—dc21   98-3025
                                                       CIP

♲ Printed on recycled paper

Contents

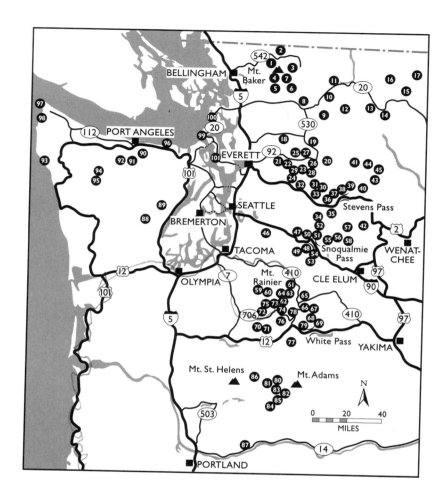

Stevens Pass Highway: West 93

Key to Symbols

Day hikes. These are hikes that can be completed in a single day. While most trips allow camping, few require it.

Backpack trips. These are hikes whose length or difficulty makes camping out either necessary or recommended for most families.

Easy trails. These are relatively short, smooth, gentle trails suitable for small children or first-time hikers.

Moderate trails. Most of these are a total of 2 to 4 miles long and feature more than 500 feet of elevation gain. The trails may be rough and uneven. Hikers should wear lug-soled boots and be sure to carry the Ten Essentials (explained later).

Difficult trails. These are often rough and involve considerable elevation gain or distance. They are suitable for older or experienced children. Lug-soled boots and the Ten Essentials are standard equipment.

Hikable season(s). The best times of year to hike each trail are indicated by the following symbols: flower—spring; sun—summer; leaf—fall; snowflake—winter.

Driving directions. These paragraphs tell you how to get to the trailheads.

Turnarounds. These are places, mostly along moderate or difficult trails, where families can cut their hikes short yet still have satisfying outings. Turnarounds usually offer picnic opportunities, views, or special natural attractions.

Cautions. These mark potential hazards—cliffs, stream crossings, and the like—where close supervision of children is strongly recommended.

Acknowledgments

For his constant help, encouragement, willingness to check trail and road maps, and loyal support, I wish to thank Ira Spring.

John Spring scouted and double-checked many of the hikes.

Jerry Franklin advised me and gave me help with ecological information.

Harvey Manning read the whole manuscript twice and made many helpful suggestions.

I feel fortunate to have such knowledgeable, good friends.

—Joan Burton

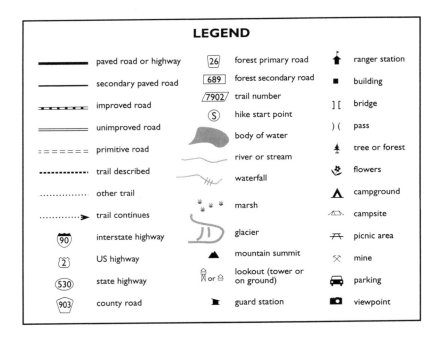

LEGEND

paved road or highway	26	forest primary road	ranger station
secondary paved road	689	forest secondary road	building
improved road	7902	trail number	bridge
unimproved road	S	hike start point	pass
primitive road		body of water	tree or forest
trail described		river or stream	flowers
other trail		waterfall	campground
trail continues		marsh	campsite
interstate highway 90		glacier	picnic area
US highway 2		mountain summit	mine
state highway 530		lookout (tower or on ground)	parking
county road 903		guard station	viewpoint

Foreword

When I heard that my father (Ira Spring) was taking the photographs for a children's hiking guide, I was thrilled. I consider my father and my mother to be bona fide experts on the subject. They took me on my first hike when I was five months old, taught me to hike the same day I learned to walk, kept me interested when I was a teenager, and encouraged me to set out on my own as an adult.

It has been quite a few years since I was a little child, trailing along after my parents, walking through rainstorms and crying because I was promised two nights out in the snow and only got one. However, I still remember my feelings when I had short legs and everybody else had long ones.

Hiking was fun because my parents told me it was fun, and I was a very trusting child. And my parents worked to make it fun for me.

First, we always had a destination. I knew when my feet hit the trail how far I had to go, and woe and misfortune to anyone who suggested that we turn back before reaching some wonderful lake, the tip-top of a real, but probably quite small mountain or, best of all, an old lookout that was sure to be strewn with treasures.

Second, I always had the company of my older brother and maybe a cousin or a friend. This was very clever of my parents because we competed with each other to see who could go the fastest the longest. By myself, with just my two parents for company, I would have gotten bored and quickly become exhausted.

Third, my parents always carried incredible treats whenever we hiked. At home we never were given big chunks of chocolate or any kind of candy at all that I can remember. However, on the trail, they carried "energy food" and, believe me, my brother and I fell for that trick quite happily. "Five more switchbacks and we take an energy stop" would have us running up the trail as fast as we could.

There are a lot of unpleasant things about hiking that bother little children. My parents took care to make sure that these things did not ruin our experience. They wanted us to want to go hiking again, so we were not asked to become macho woodsmen overnight. I can remember being carried on my father's shoulders through nettle patches, being lifted over logs, being taught to make slapping mosquitoes a game, and being fed dinner in a warm tent when it was raining.

As soon as we were old enough, my parents liberated my brother and me. We were allowed to go ahead as long as we stuck together and stayed on the trail. This was the best. Together we never had time to be tired. Our first aim was to get as far ahead of our parents as possible. Then we proceeded to have a great time, playing at being motorcycles, trucks, or race cars as we zoomed up the switchbacks.

Looking back, I would say that my parents' most effective ploy was to have only one day pack for my brother and me. When my brother realized that he was to have the pack and I wasn't, he was very proud and I was green with jealousy. They could dump pounds of stuff in that pack and still my brother carried it, just because he knew how badly I wanted to.

And, can you believe this? As soon as my parents let us go ahead, he would let me carry it for miles as long as I promised not to tell! It wasn't until I was nine and had read *Tom Sawyer* that I finally caught on, and my parents had to buy me a pack of my very own to get me to carry anything.

Maybe the most important thing my parents did was never to complain in my hearing. If the trail was bad, if they were cold, tired, or just out of sorts, we never knew it. My parents were excellent role models on the trail. I didn't know it was okay to complain when things were really bad. After all, I had never heard them complain.

One day my mother nearly got sick when she saw me pull off my socks, bloodstained almost to the ankles from bleeding blisters. This was really unfortunate because the best thing about hiking was that it got my brother and me out of doing our four hours of work around the house before we were set free to play. So you can understand that I was devastated when my mother decided that I would have to stay home until the blisters on my feet healed to her satisfaction. I got blisters on my hands from working in the garden before I was allowed back on the trail with new boots.

Now that I am grown up, carry a heavier pack than my parents, and sometimes slow down enough to hike with them, I'm not sure if being given a taste for the outdoors was a good thing. By the time I was a teenager I was hooked on the outdoors; now I'm addicted. My house is filled with tents, skis, hiking boots, climbing ropes, and bicycles. And holding a steady job is not to my taste at all. Rather than sit at some old desk, I would much rather tighten my belt, load up the pack, and head for the outdoors whenever I want. It's all my parents' fault.

Vicky Spring, Former Kid

Introduction

Hiking with little children requires planning, patience, psychology, strategy, and, at some points, outright bribery. Is it worth it? Of course it is! You, the parents, can introduce them to the outdoors, have some "family time," and hike to places you've wanted to see anyway. With luck your children may grow up to love the mountains, rivers, lakes, and beaches and be willing to carry their own packs.

Read on for some of the strategies that worked with my children when they were young, susceptible, and believed everything I told them.

1. **Appoint a "First Leader."** I rotated this official designation among my three children. Somehow, being tagged "First Leader" imparted status—and extra energy, at least for a while. Unspoken competition between brothers and sisters can be a powerful motivating force (which is why we did not encourage walking sticks). It's a good idea to agree in advance on a point at which the official title rotates again.

Family hiking Glacier Basin Trail (Hike 62)

2. **Frequent "energy stops."** As in, "When we get to that creek ahead, we'll have an energy stop, where we'll have some . . . ."
3. **Energy food.** Candy, fruit, or a favorite family treat. Never *called* candy, and always rationed out in tiny increments to prolong its effectiveness. Popeye's spinach comes to mind.
4. **Take a friend along.** Aches, pains, and complaints are often forgotten when there is a companion the child's own age along on the hike. The child will not want to look slow or tired in front of the friend, and a little friendly rivalry, not unlike sibling rivalry, won't hurt.
5. **Praise, praise, praise.** Only a parent knows how thick to spread this, but positive reinforcement may have the most durable results of all. When my sister and I were eight and nine, my father took us to Melakwa Lake. Over 40 years later, I still remember what a fuss he made over how strong and fast we were. His praise was probably vast exaggeration, but consider the effect it had.
6. **Patience.** This means taking time, if necessary, to inspect every creek, throw sticks and stones over bridges, and look up for birds and down at animal tracks. If parents want to get home (or into a campsite) before dark, they must plan ahead for a pace to fit the child's ability and attention span. Try not to look at your watch any more than necessary. If you keep winding it and shaking it, the child will suspect you are not having as much fun as he or she is.

How to Use This Book

Most of the hikes described in this guidebook are in the Cascade Range or the Olympic Mountains. A few are found in nearby foothills and lowlands. The hikes are numbered consecutively but grouped by the major highways from which they are accessible. This arrangement makes it easy for readers to find the hikes they want. See the table of contents for a complete list of hikes arranged by highway.

Each hike description includes (1) a block summarizing important information about each hike, (2) symbols for features of special interest, and (3) the description itself, which tells you what to expect, how to get to the trail, and where to go from there.

Hikes are rated easy, moderate, or difficult. These ratings are only approximations. I tried to factor in distances, elevation gains, and trail conditions, but even those are not altogether objective criteria. I thought of giving minimum age levels for trails but found that to be even more subjective. A trail that one five year old is capable of hiking may be too difficult for another. In any case, the most important factor is motivation. If kids want to hike somewhere, energy and stamina will follow. The reverse is also true: If children do not want to go on, any trail at any time can be too steep and too long.

The great majority of hikes can be completed in one day, but camping opportunities are plentiful and have been noted for families who are more adventurous or experienced. Some trips are primarily overnight excursions, but beginning sections can make good day hikes; it is not always necessary to walk the entire distance.

In the same way, many hikes that are rated moderate or difficult contain shorter, easier sections that make excellent day hikes in their own right. So if you want a shorter outing, don't restrict your search only to those hikes I have rated easy. Instead, scan the more difficult trips for what I call *turnarounds,* which are marked in both margin and text by a special symbol (see "Key to Symbols"). Turnarounds are satisfying destinations that make fine picnic spots and feature scenic views or other natural attractions. You can turn around at a turnaround and feel well satisfied with your hike.

Short Legs can hike along with Long Ones

I have also indicated the months during which each trail is free of snow. This can vary from year to year. Early or late in the season, when there may be some doubt about current snow conditions, call the local ranger station in the area where you want to hike.

Hikers venturing into wild or otherwise roadless areas should carry a current topographic map and compass (most outdoor-equipment stores stock them) and know how to use them. Green Trails topographic maps and U.S. Forest Service or National Park Service maps are listed for each hike.

Maps

Topographic maps show terrain and altitude by means of contour lines and provide a fairly accurate way of gauging trail steepness and general terrain features. The Green Trails maps are one of two types of topographic maps widely used by local hikers. The second type is published by the United States Geologic Survey (USGS). Though widely available, many USGS maps are out-of-date, and they do not give recent road or trail numbers. Green Trails maps are listed because they are updated more often and show all existing trails in green, features that are particularly important for beginning hikers.

An appropriate U.S. Forest Service or National Park Service map is also listed for each hike. These maps generally do not show contours, but they do give the names and numbers of all access roads, which no other types of map do. This information is particularly important for hikers venturing into an area for the first time.

Numbering of National Forest roads has become rather complicated. Major forest roads are identified by two- or four-digit numbers, but those designating minor roads may have seven digits. In such numbers, the first three digits indicate the main road, and the remainder identify a particular spur leading off the main one. Be sure the map you carry is as up-to-date as possible.

Road mileage is expressed in decimals rounded to the nearest tenth of a mile to correspond to odometer readings. Trail mileage is expressed in fractions because decimals imply a greater degree of accuracy than is possible or practical on trails. Even so, all mileages are as accurate as possible.

What to Take

Boots

Rocky, uneven trails can subject small feet and shoes to more wear and tear than they are designed to handle. On many of the shorter, gentler trails in this book, running shoes or other sneakers may be adequate, but on longer, steeper trails or when the hiker is carrying a heavy pack, such footwear may not offer enough protection. Boots are a must for extended day hikes and all backpack trips. Unfortunately, boots for children are expensive—especially since children's feet somehow seem to grow even faster than the rest of them. But there's hope for the budget.

I bought one pair of good boots for the first child, passed them down the line, and traded outgrown hand-me-downs with other families. Some outdoor equipment stores will take back usable children's boots for their rental trade and offer a price based on their value, which can be applied to the next pair.

When buying boots (for children or adults), keep in mind that boots that don't fit properly can make their owner utterly miserable (so can wet tennis shoes). It is therefore important to make sure your child's boots fit properly. They should be snug enough to prevent chafing but not so tight that they pinch toes. After buying your child a pair of boots, have him or her wear them inside the house for several days before using them outdoors. This will not only help to break in the boots but will often reveal poorly fitting ones while it's still possible to return them. Usually, an ill-fitting pair can be returned for full value. Even well-fitting boots, however, need to be broken in before they are suitable for an extended hike. Otherwise, blisters are virtually certain. For that reason, children forced to hike far in stiff new boots may never willingly hike anywhere again.

Packs

Child-size packs and bags are available at most backpacking stores. Parents can calculate how soon they will be outgrown and how much use they will get. Sometimes, packs are a source of rivalry among little children, who are likely to gauge another child's load by size alone. Unless a child has his or her own pack, good parental strategy is to fill an adult day pack with the child's extra clothing, take a tuck in the straps, and allow him or her to appear to be carrying an enormous load. This is a surefire morale booster for a kid. Other children on the trail are not likely to heft one another's packs, so no one but the parents will know how much it holds.

The Ten Essentials

Over the years, The Mountaineers has compiled a list of ten items that should be taken on every hike. These Ten Essentials not only make your trip more comfortable but equip you to cope with emergencies caused by bad weather, injury, or other unforeseen circumstances.

1. **Extra clothing.** Weather changes or an unplanned swim mean trouble if there are no changes of clothing.
2. **Extra food.** Carry enough food so that if your hike lasts longer than you expect, you and your children won't be hungry.
3. **Sunglasses.** Bright sun on snow or water can be blinding.
4. **Knife.** Useful in countless situations.
5. **Fire-starting candle or chemical fuel.** If you should unexpectedly have to stay overnight, you will want to build a fire.
6. **First-aid kit.** Keep it well supplied and hope you won't need it.
7. **Matches in a waterproof container.** No fire is possible without them. Look for waterproof matches in hiking outfitter stores.
8. **Flashlight.** Imagine walking down a trail in the dark with little children—without a light.
9. **Map.** Be sure you have the correct and current map for your hike.
10. **Compass.** Know how to use it with your map to orient yourself.

Children require a few extra essentials; the items mentioned below are ones I found useful:

1. **Child-safe protection from bugs and sun.** Mosquitoes, no-see-ums, gnats, deerflies, and sunburn can make anyone miserable.

Obviously, you will need protection from insects and sun. But chemical products designed for adult skin—particularly sun creams with high screen factors—may be too harsh for children. Take the time to check and test untried products before you leave home. Don't assume they will be safe if there is even a possibility of an allergic reaction—2 miles away from the car and 50 miles from home is no place to find out.

2. **Extra bug protection.** Be sure each child has a long-sleeved shirt to wear when bugs attack. There may even be times when a cap, gloves, and long pants will be needed. Repellent helps some but is overrated. Give the kids (and yourselves) personal "habitats"—a 6-foot length of no-see-um netting for each camper, light enough to wad up in a pocket and large enough to cover the head and be tucked under the bottom at dinner time.

3. **Allergy and sting medication.** If your child is allergic to bee or wasp stings, be sure to carry the appropriate medications prescribed or recommended by your physician.

4. **Extra first-aid kit supplies.** Your first-aid kit should also contain any other special medicines or supplies your child may need, such as extra moleskin for blisters on tender feet, extra toilet paper, and some baking soda to plaster on nettle or other stings.

5. **Swimming gear.** Do not encourage children to go into lakes in jeans, because wet jeans can become extremely cold and uncomfortable later. Carry shorts or bathing suits for wading and swimming. Also, hidden hazards lie on lake bottoms. Carry an extra pair of tennis shoes for the child to wade in, to protect against sharp rocks and sticks buried in muddy lake bottoms.

Food

Food is a matter of family preference, of course. My family enjoyed meals whose ingredients came from the grocery store rather than from sporting goods shops. Freeze-dried foods are not only more expensive, but also less tasty than familiar home favorites. Don't experiment with unknown, gourmet foods on a camping trip with children. Comfort foods are one-pot meals—such as stew, chili, and chicken and noodles—that children know from home. Day hike foods should be combinations of nuts, fruit, candies, raisins, cheese, and crackers that are easy to carry without being crushed in the pack and that impart energy.

Safety

Backcountry travel, even on day hikes, entails unavoidable risks that every hiker assumes and must be aware of and respect. The fact that a trail is described in this book is not an indication that it will be safe for you. The trips presented here vary in difficulty and in the amount and kind of preparation needed for you to enjoy them safely. Some routes may have changed or conditions on them may have deteriorated since this book was written. Also, of course, especially in mountain areas, conditions can change even from day to day, owing to weather and other factors. A trip that is safe in good weather or for a well-conditioned, properly equipped hiker may be completely unsafe for someone else or for anyone in adverse weather.

You can minimize your risks by being knowledgeable, prepared, and alert. There is not space in this book for a general treatise on wilderness safety, but there are a number of good books and public courses on the subject, and you should take advantage of them to increase your knowledge. Just as important, you should always be aware of your own limitations and the conditions existing when and where you are traveling. If conditions are dangerous or if you are not prepared to deal with them safely, change your plans! It is better to have wasted a few days than to be the subject of a wilderness rescue.

Mount Rainier from Pinnacle Saddle (Hike 76)

These warnings are not intended to keep you out of the wilderness. Most people enjoy safe trips through the backcountry every year. However, one element of the beauty, freedom, and excitement of the wilderness is the presence of risks that do not confront us at home. When you travel in the backcountry, you assume those risks. They can be met safely but only if you exercise your own independent good judgment and common sense.

Water

Drinking water is another cause for concern and preparation. Do not trust that streams and lakes will supply you with pure water. Most mountain water is safe, but much is not, and there's no way to tell. If the trail is popular and the lake is crowded, be suspicious. Carry a canteen or plastic bottle of water or flavored drinks for the trail. (If you carry in cans of juice or pop, be sure to carry out empties.) Cooking water must be boiled at least 20 minutes. Iodine tablets or water filtering devices also guarantee pure water.

Hypothermia

Most of the mountain lakes described here are very cold, and weather conditions in the mountains can change abruptly. Parents should be aware of the hazards of hypothermia and carry extra clothing and perhaps a thermos of cocoa or hot soup. Because of their relatively small body size, little children are vulnerable to hypothermia sooner than are adults exposed to the same conditions. In fact, a parent may not even recognize the symptoms in children. Children with first-stage hypothermia can be listless, whiny, and unwilling to cooperate, long before physical signs, like shivering, start to appear. Since these symptoms can also occur on hikes when children are only tired, bored, or hungry, it is important to rule out hypothermia before assuming some other cause. Early morning, late afternoon and evening, and periods of cool, overcast weather are times to be particularly alert to your child's behavior and to take immediate steps to rewarm him or her if appropriate.

Good Outdoor Manners

Hiking families have an obligation to teach children good outdoor manners. The hiker's motto should be "Leave trails and campsites as clean as or cleaner than you found them." Parents can set an example by cleaning up other people's messy camps and by carrying out or burning leftover trash. Do not leave old plastic tarps behind for the next camping family. They blow around, are quickly ripped and tattered, and add to the litter. In fact, anything you can carry in, you can carry out. Think about how your family feels at seeing old tin cans, bottles, and plastic containers in places they have hiked miles to see.

Tell children they must not drop candy or gum wrappers, orange peels, or peanut or egg shells. These things take a long time to break down, and petrified orange peels are not an archaeological find we want to leave to posterity. Also, don't bury garbage; it doesn't stay covered for long.

Carry out cans, aluminum foil, and disposable diapers. One way to handle such materials in parents' packs is to include several zippable plastic bags for garbage, wet clothing, and the things children find along the way that they want to bring home.

Teach your children to dispose of toilet paper properly. Burying it with their stools used to be acceptable, but little creatures dig up the paper and strew it about. I've seen campsites so littered with toilet paper, the prospect of camping there was disgusting. If you have a campfire, burn toilet paper or put it in plastic bags and pack it out. Parents should check their children's toilet area after use to be sure they have the technique down and that the area is usable by the next visitors.

Dogs are permitted but not welcomed on national forest trails. They are absolutely not allowed in national parks. Though children may love day hiking with their pet, its presence in a backpacking campsite may impact birds and small animals and annoy other campers who came partly to get away from domestic animals.

Crime

Theft, both in camps and from parked cars at trailheads, has become a major problem. So many hikers' cars have been vandalized that wise hikers arrange to be dropped off and picked up from trailheads. If you must leave a parked car for several days, don't tempt thieves by leaving expensive clothing and gear in plain view. Tell a Forest Service official, if you can, that you will be parked at such-and-such a trailhead for a duration of time and you would appreciate having someone check your car during patrols of the area.

Wilderness Regulations

With the increasingly heavy use of Washington's backcountry, many parks, wilderness areas, and national forests have instituted permit requirements or user fees that affect both day hikers and backpackers. Whether you need a permit depends on where you are going and how long you will stay.

As this is being written, overnight backcountry trips in Mount Rainier, North Cascades, and Olympic national parks require a permit while day trips do not. Several of Washington's federally designated Wilderness Areas require permits for both day use and overnight stays. Permit requirements for national parks and wilderness areas are listed in the information blocks that precede the hikes.

You should keep in mind, however, that permit requirements can and do change and that information on the permit status of national forest areas has not been included. It is always best to call the pertinent ranger district office or information center (also listed in the information block) to determine the situation at the time you wish to hike.

Permits can be obtained at ranger stations and national park information centers as well as at many trailheads and some sporting goods stores. Fees are generally nominal.

Another regulation to be aware of concerns party size. In designated wilderness areas and national parks, the maximum number of visitors in any one group is twelve.

Parental Attitudes

Children take their cues from grown-ups about how safe and nonthreatening the woods and mountains are. If you are comfortable hiking in diverse places and weather conditions, your children usually will feel secure and comfortable too. That is not to say you might not have some perfectly horrid experiences. My youngest cut a tooth in the middle of the night once and cried incessantly while we hiked out, reached the car, and drove almost a hundred miles home.

My daughter Carol says she remembers riding piggyback or in a forerunner of today's child carrier and putting her hands over my eyes because it was fun when I would stop and say I couldn't see. She also remembers untreated boots and soaking clothes that got wet and cold in the rain and on the wet brush alongside the path when she was First Leader.

On the other hand, we did have some triumphs. As a family recreational activity, hiking became an important way to give my children a sense of their ability to succeed at difficult but satisfying undertakings. One day hike that gave my two younger children, at twelve and thirteen, a real sense of achievement was the trail to Camp Muir. I do not recommend this hike for little children. It is steep, arduous, long, and, in fog, treacherous. But on a beautiful, windy day in late July, we started up from Paradise with boots, day packs, and wind gear. The kids knew my husband and I had each climbed Mount Rainier and that this was the way to the climbers' high camp.

Five hours went by—all spent switchbacking up steep snow, the guide hut always receding, like a mirage, before us. The children were weary and discouraged at how far and how steep the hike was turning out to be. We developed an unspoken unity of purpose. We were going to make Camp Muir—together. Dick, my son, would go ahead for a while then wait for us. Carol, who was small but wiry, would lag behind, discouraged, then surge ahead. We talked about what the summit climb is like, and the kids said later that those conversations and the collective family pride in achievement meant much to them. They knew that sometime, somehow, we were going to make it.

When we finally climbed over the Muir rocks to the coffin-shaped nests there, the wind was fierce. We hunkered down in a nest to escape the wind and ate our lunch, rejoicing. The kids had met an important test successfully. What better gifts can parents give than self-sufficiency and self-confidence?

A Note About Safety

Safety is an important concern in all outdoor activities. No guidebook can alert you to every hazard or anticipate the limitations of every reader. Therefore, the descriptions of roads, trails, routes, and natural features in this book are not representations that a particular place or excursion will be safe for your party. When you follow any of the routes described in this book, you assume responsibility for your own safety. Under normal conditions, such excursions require the usual attention to traffic, road and trail conditions, weather, terrain, the capabilities of your party, and other factors. Keeping informed on current conditions and exercising common sense are the keys to a safe, enjoyable outing.

The Mountaineers

Coleman Glacier from Heliotrope Ridge Trail

Mount Baker Highway

State Route 542

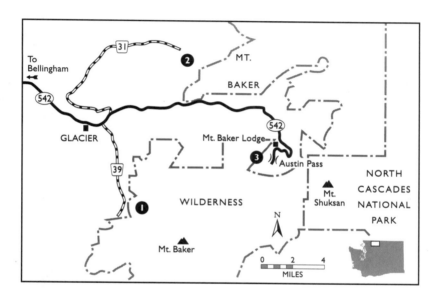

1. Heliotrope Ridge

Type: Day hike or backpack
Difficulty: Moderate for children
Hikable: August–September
One way: 2¾ miles
High point: 6,000 feet
Elevation gain: 2,300 feet
Maps: Green Trails No. 13 Mount Baker; U.S. Forest Service Mount Baker–Snoqualmie
Information: Glacier Public Service Center (360)599-2714

This hike provides a child with a chance to glimpse alpine wonders—
to see a glacier headwall and its savage crevasses and to hear the
groaning and cracking sounds of an icefall on a shoulder of Mount
Baker. Many summit climbers use this route, so children may admire
them at close range as well. While experienced hikers travel this route
from early July, because three creek crossings are very difficult during
the high-water periods of snowmelt, it is best to wait until late summer
to take children.

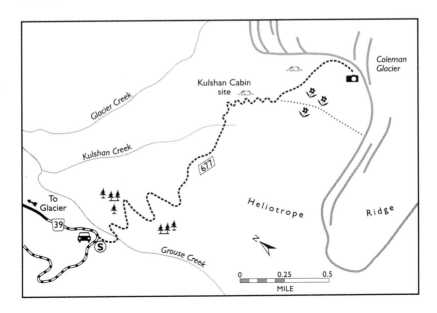

Mountain daisy

Drive north on I-5 past Bellingham to Exit 255 then east on Mount Baker Highway 542 to the town of Glacier. About 1 mile beyond, turn right on Glacier Creek road No. 39 and follow it 8 miles to the trailhead parking lot, elevation 3,700 feet.

The rough, well-used trail gains 1,000 feet in 2 switchbacking miles. At 1¾ miles, you cross the first difficult streams. At 2 miles, you pass the site of the old Kulshan Cabin and break out of timber into open meadows and all-summer snowfields at the beginning of Heliotrope Ridge. At ¾ mile more is a young moraine overlooking the Coleman Glacier, elevation 6,000 feet.

Coleman Glacier has been advancing in recent years—that is, the ice from high on the mountain is pushing down faster than the warm air at lower elevations can melt it. The aggressive Coleman frequently obliges visitors by putting on some sort of show. And even if it doesn't stage a noisy avalanche, icefall, or spectacular panorama of broken crevasses, you can depend on hearing the marmots and pikas whistling messages to their families. Look for marmot burrows, where they retreat for safety and where they hibernate, usually from September to April. Pikas like rock slides, rather than burrows. These small members of the rabbit family spend the winter in rock slides, nibbling on the hay they gathered and cured the previous summer. Scan rock slides for "cony haystacks" of succulent meadow plants left to cure in the sun.

The ridge has several possible car campsites if you want to stay.

2. Excelsior Mountain

Type: Day hike or backpack
Difficulty: Moderate for children
Hikable: Mid-July–September
One way: 3 miles
High point: 5,699 feet
Elevation gain: 1,200 feet
Maps: Green Trails No. 13 Mount Baker; U.S. Forest Service Mount Baker–Snoqualmie
Information: Glacier Public Service Center (360)599-2714

My children call this the "Sound of Music Mountain" because its alpine meadows and spectacular views of Mount Baker, Mount Shuksan, and peaks across the border in Canada reminded them of the movie scenery. The mountain is actually named for a long-ago mine called the Great Excelsior. The trail is neither steep nor gentle, gaining 500 feet a mile. It can be very muddy when the snow is melting or after several days of rain.

Drive north on I-5 to Exit 255 and then east on Mount Baker Highway 542 to Glacier; continue 2 miles beyond to Canyon Creek road No. 31. Turn left and drive 15 miles to the parking lot and trail No. 625, elevation 4,200 feet.

Hike through lush woodland for 1 mile to a junction with the Canyon Ridge trail. Keep right and continue past the two small, marshy but picturesque Damfino Lakes (so named because when two early

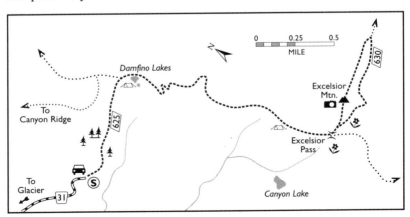

Excelsior Mountain Trail and Mount Baker

travelers came here, one asked, "What lakes are these?" and the other said, "Damfino").

At 2½ miles from the road, you enter superb green meadows and cross a stream where the last drops quit flowing by mid-August. To the right are campsites without views. At 3 miles, you reach Excelsior Pass, elevation 5,400 feet, and the first view of Mount Baker across the deep Nooksack Valley. It is a wonderful place to have lunch, but the best is a bit farther. Either follow the trail contouring around the mountain or take the steep, boot-beaten shortcut another ½ mile to the peak itself, 5,699-foot Excelsior Mountain. Be careful not to stumble—the views are so breathtaking one may forget about feet. Mount Baker, Mount Shuksan, and the Canadian Border Peaks loom large enough that children may ask if they can stay and climb them tomorrow. In settled weather, you can sleep on the summit where the fire-lookout cabin used to be. Camping here is unforgettable: Imagine moonlight on two glaciated mountains and settlement lights on the shores of Puget Sound.

3. Chain Lakes

Type:	Day hike or backpack
Difficulty:	Easy to moderate for children
Hikable:	Late July–October
One way:	1¾ miles plus
High point:	5,200 feet
Elevation gain:	400 feet
Maps:	Green Trails No. 14 Mount Shuksan; U.S. Forest Service Mount Baker–Snoqualmie
Information:	Glacier Public Service Center (360)599-2714

This group of four alpine lakes has enough scenic campsites with views to accommodate many families. If you wish, you can move camp from lake to lake along the chain and enjoy different views and different settings each day. Expect blueberries in August and September and fish in Hayes and Arbuthnot lakes anytime.

Drive east on Mount Baker Highway 542 some 60 miles from Bellingham to the Mount Baker Lodge and continue from there on a possibly snowy paved road to its end at Kulshan Ridge, elevation 5,100 feet. (The road is usually open in mid-July but some years may not thaw out until August or September.) The trailhead is to the left of the Table Mountain trail on the Mount Baker side of the parking lot.

The trail drops a few feet, then contours around the side of Table

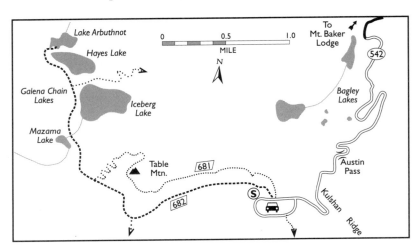

Mountain, with views of parkland meadows below and Mount Baker above. Columnar andesite formations of ancient lava flows alternate along the trail with horizontal layers of 10,000-year-old ash and pumice; those from different eruptions exhibit different colors. Tell the kids the layers are like squeezed fillings in sandwiches. They may not be impressed when you tell them much of this ash was blown out "only" 10,000 years ago, but their interest may perk up when they learn Mount Baker is thought capable of exploding again at any time, just like Mount St. Helens.

At the highest point on the way around Table Mountain, the trail descends a steep snowfield that lasts to late summer. If there is a safe runout below, sliding may be in order, but tennis shoes will get wet.

The first of the lakes, little Mazama, is at 1¾ miles. In another ¼ mile, beautiful Iceberg Lake calls to you to stop for lunch, at least. Continue on and down less than 1 mile to Hayes and Arbuthnot lakes, where some of the shores are black volcanic sand. A loop back out to the road from here is possible but is not recommended for children, so turn around and retrace your steps.

Mazama Lake, smallest of the four Chain Lakes

Mount Baker from Dock Butte

North Cascades Highway: West

State Route 20

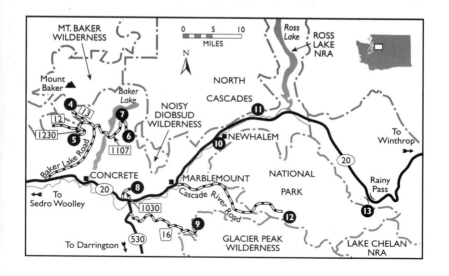

4. Railroad Grade

Type: Day hike or backpack
Difficulty: Moderate to difficult for children
Hikable: Mid-July–October
One way: 2½ miles
High point: 4,560 feet
Elevation gain: 1,300 feet
Maps: Green Trails No. 46 Hamilton; U.S. Forest Service Mount Baker–Snoqualmie
Information: Mount Baker Ranger District (360)856-5700

The fascinating ramble from subalpine meadows up to a moraine of the Easton Glacier will delight older children. Families may stop and camp at any point along the way to enjoy views of Mount Baker and, in season, pick blueberries.

Drive North Cascades Highway 20 east 14.6 miles past Sedro Woolley and turn left on the Baker Lake Road passing Grandy Lake. At 12.5 miles from Highway 20, just beyond the Rocky Creek bridge, turn left on road No. 12 and go 3 miles to a junction. Go right on road No. 13 for 6 miles to its end, elevation 3,200 feet.

The trail begins in subalpine forest, crossing Sulphur Creek immediately, entering meadows at ⅓ mile and passing the ruins of two old shelter cabins on the right. Blueberries and huckleberries in late August and September are superb.

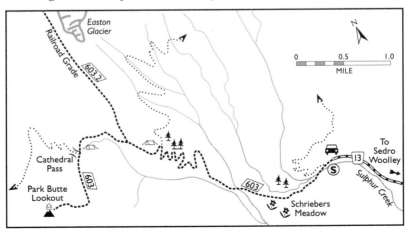

Mount Baker reflected in a small tarn on Park Butte

Crossings of several creeks at 1 mile can be difficult when the snowmelt is running, turning them into torrents. Then comes 1 mile of steep switchbacks through old-growth timber.

Energy stops may be required for jelly beans, peppermints, or berries. At approximately 2½ miles, the grade eases and the trail enters large meadows with close-up views of Mount Baker and the Easton Glacier.

Campsites are numerous. For explorations, go ¼ mile to a junction. The left fork climbs to the lookout on Park Butte, maintained by volunteers. The right climbs to the snout of the Easton Glacier and its parallel moraines, so neatly heaped up and with such uniform crests they appear ready to have railroad tracks laid on them.

5. Blue Lake

Type: Day hike or backpack
Difficulty: Easy for children
Hikable: July–October
One way: 1 mile
High point: 4,300 feet
Elevation gain: 300 feet
Maps: Green Trails No. 45 Hamilton; U.S. Forest ServiceMount Baker–Snoqualmie
Information: Mount Baker Ranger District (360)856-5700

An easy walk to an alpine jewel of a lake. Families will find the distance and the elevation gain slight enough for young children.

Drive North Cascades Highway 20 east 14.5 miles past Sedro Woolley, turn left on the Baker Lake Road for 12.5 miles, and just past the Rocky Creek Bridge turn left on road No. 12. Keep left at the junction with road No. 13, and at 6.6 miles from Baker Lake Road, turn left on road No. 1230 for another 3.8 miles to the trailhead, elevation 4,000 feet.

Trail No. 604 leads uphill from the parking lot, crosses a low saddle, and within 100 feet reaches a junction. The left fork is a rough up-and-down waste-of-time short-cut to the lake. Keep right on a good trail, climbing in a long ½ mile to the junction with the Dock Butte trail. Go left, contouring to the lake. The lake shore is steep. The best wading for kids is near the outlet.

A short second or alternative hike is up Dock Butte, accessible by the right fork back at the second junction. The trail climbs ½ mile, past meadows, ponds, and gorgeous views. From this point the views increase but so does the steepness. The widest views, of course, are from the old lookout site atop Dock Butte, elevation 5,210 feet.

Gray jay

Blue Lake

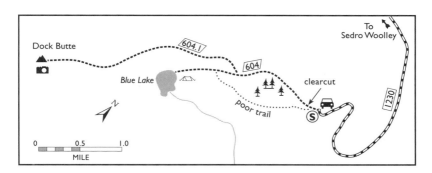

6. Anderson-Watson Lakes

Type: Day hike or backpack
Difficulty: Difficult for children
Hikable: July–October
One way: 2½ miles
High point: 4,700 feet
Elevation gain: 1,200 feet
Maps: Green Trails No. 46 Lake Shannon; U.S. Forest Service Mount Baker–Snoqualmie
Information: Mount Baker Ranger District (360)856-5700

These five very popular alpine lakes are surrounded by acres of meadows, cliffs, and gorgeous scenery and offer families diverse opportunities to camp, fish, wade, and explore. The views of Mount Baker, Mount Watson, and Anderson Butte can tempt hikers to go on and on, although trails are rough, sometimes very steep, and filled with roots and rocks.

Drive North Cascades Highway 20 east of Sedro Woolley 14.5 miles and go left on the Baker Lake–Grandy Lake Road. Enter the Mount Baker–Snoqualmie National Forest at 12 miles, continue approximately 2 miles more, and turn right on the Baker Dam–Baker Campground road.

In 1 mile, drive over the Upper Baker Dam (children will enjoy peering down the face of the dam to Lake Shannon below) and in 2 miles, go left on gravel road No. 1107. Follow this scenic road 9-plus miles to a junction and go left on road No. (1107)002, steep and rough in places, to the trailhead, 1.5 miles from the dam, elevation 4,300 feet.

The first ⅛ mile of the trail is very steep (an omen of things to come). There are very large old-growth Douglas firs along the way, one of which has been felled and flattened on one side for 40 feet to become a part of the trail, a child's delight. The way reaches the ridge and then tilts steeply upward, sometimes on good tread and other times on roots and rock. At 1 mile, pass the side trail to Anderson Butte, site of a former fire lookout. The main trail loses 100 feet and

then climbs through meadows to the high point at 4,700 feet before dropping steeply to a junction in about 2 miles.

Here the trail splits. The left fork climbs 150 feet over a ridge, enters the Noisy-Diobsud Wilderness, and drops steeply to more meadows and the shore of glacier-carved Upper Watson Lake, at 4,500 feet. Lower Watson Lake, the larger of the two, is a short ½ mile

Upper Watson Lake

farther. Campsites here have views of the lake and of the glaciers on
Bacon Peak.

The right fork is a rough, up-and-down ½ mile to Lower Anderson
Lake, at 4,500 feet; you'll find campsites on both sides and a view
of Mount Baker from the meadows. The lake is small enough, like
the baby bear's chair, to be "just right" for small children.

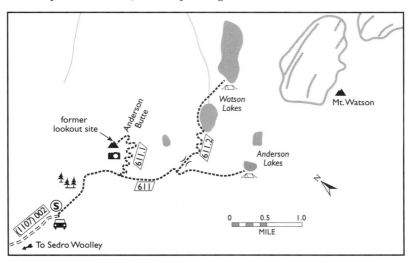

7. East Bank of Baker Lake

Type: Day hike or backpack
Difficulty: Moderate for children
Hikable: May–November
One way: 1½ miles
High point: 970 feet
Elevation gain: (on return) 250 feet
Maps: Green Trails No. 46 Lake Shannon; U.S. Forest Service Mount Baker–Snoqualmie recreation map
Information: Mount Baker Ranger District (360)856-5700

"Where is the lake?" was the comment written in the register. The hiker did not go far enough. The answer is, "At the campground on the lake shore." This trail was started in 1980 and will eventually be a 12-mile link with the Baker River Trail.

Drive North Cascades Highway 20 east of Sedro Woolley 14.5 miles and go left on Baker Lake–Grandy Road. Enter the Mount Baker–Snoqualmie National Forest at 12 miles. Continue approximately 2 miles more and turn right on the Baker Dam–Baker Campground road. In 1 mile, cross the top of the Upper Baker Dam (children will love looking straight down its face) and in 2 miles go left on gravel road No. 1107. Follow this road another 1.5 miles to the East Bank trailhead, elevation 970 feet.

Walk down first through second-growth timber and then between immense old-growth cedar trees and stumps, some with cavities

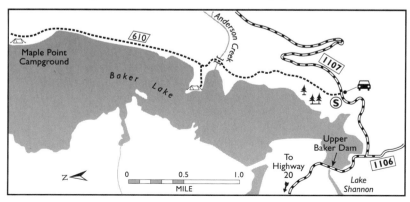

Mount Baker from campsite on East Bank of Baker Lake Trail

children can slip into. Moss hangs from every tree and carpets the ground. Wooden bridges fringed with maidenhair ferns cover little streams. Look for a first view of the lake at about ½ mile. From that point on, the lake is never out of view for long.

At about 1 mile, cross Anderson Creek on a bridge and in another ¼ mile reach a junction. Two miles farther is the Maple Point Campground. Go left, dropping steeply to the lakeshore and excellent campsites with views of Mount Baker. Water action has undermined the shoreline so that the only good access to the water is at the farthest campsite. Unfortunately, boat campers also have access, and they do not always take out their refuse. Campers can enjoy sunset and sunrise vistas of Mount Baker and Mount Shuksan, floating serenely above the cool waters.

8. Sauk Mountain

Type: Day hike
Difficulty: Moderate to difficult for children
Hikable: Mid-July–October
One way: 2 miles
High point: 5,537 feet
Elevation gain: 1,650 feet
Maps: Green Trails No. 46 Lake Shannon; U.S.
Forest Service Mount Baker–Snoqualmie
Information: Mount Baker Ranger District (360)856-5700

Exposed switchbacks ascend a dizzyingly steep alpine meadow to panoramic views of Whitehorse Mountain, Mount Baker, and Mount Shuksan and the merging of the serpentine Sauk, Skagit, and Cascade rivers. This is not a trail for toddlers, but my children loved it when they were six, seven, and eight, and we returned to it again and again. Once one of them was bitten by a deer fly two switchbacks above me; I could hardly run uphill fast enough. She forgot about it, though, and later joyfully took her friends back up the mountain. The road goes almost to timberline, so the entire 2-mile trail is flower meadows, in season.

 Drive North Cascades Highway 20 east from Concrete to the west boundary of Rockport State Park. Turn left on road No. 1030 for 8 miles

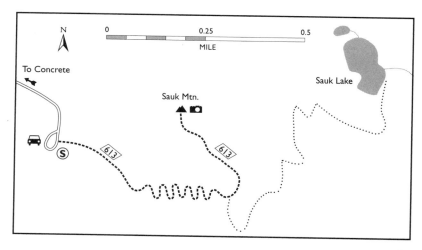

of an increasingly steep grade. If the car protests, gear down and remember, "Better the car than the hiker." At the road's end (where there is abundant parking space), elevation 3,900 feet, you may gasp at the view of the upper Skagit Valley, rivers, and North Cascades peaks.

The trail drops a bit from the parking area then reels off twenty-eight switchbacks (have the children count them—I might have missed a couple) up the super-steep slope. Watch carefully for hikers on the switchbacks above; some skip about as if alone in the world, kicking loose rocks that can come down like cannonballs. Also watch carefully to keep on the trail—thick grass and foliage obscure the edge and it is possible to step through flowers into space. **Children should be supervised here, as a step off the trail could be serious.** The higher one climbs, the greater the views. At 1½ miles, the switchbacks end on the crest of the summit ridge. The trail ascends another ½ mile along the sidehill to new views and a final rock climb to the old lookout site. Even on a foggy day there are flowery rewards; on a clear day, expect magnificence.

Flower fields on Sauk Mountain

9. Slide Lake

Type: Day hike or backpack
Difficulty: Moderate for children
Hikable: July to September
One way: 1½ mile
High point: 3,100 feet
Elevation gain: 300 feet
Map: U.S. Forest Service Mount Baker–Snoqualmie
Information: Mount Baker Ranger District (360)856-5700

Your children might call this either a frightening or a fascinating geology lesson. With a bit of help it will be easy for them to visualize a gigantic rock slide that hundreds of years ago dammed Otter Valley and formed Slide Lake. The lesson can be mixed with a cold swim on a hot day or a bit of fishing from a natural rock dam.

From I-5 north of Everett turn east at Exit 208 and take Highway 530 through Arlington and Darrington and cross the Sauk River. At 42 miles from the Interstate, just past Milepost 65, turn right on the Illabot Creek Road (No. 16). Go 20.5 miles and, just before the crossing of Otter Creek, find Slide Lake trail No. 635.

The hike is moderate to easy through old-growth trees and rocks, which youngsters will require some help to climb. Within ¼ mile, the geology lesson starts with huge moss-covered boulders topped by trees with roots that wrap around the rocks and reach the ground.

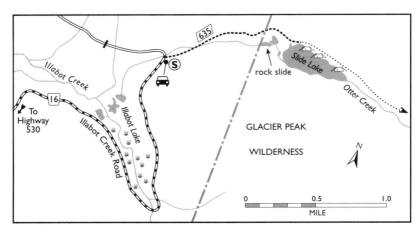

In ½ mile, the trail crosses Otter Creek, but where is it? Even at high water there is barely a trickle. The answer is that it is in underground channels through the rock slide.

At 1 mile, enter the Glacier Peak Wilderness where you'll come upon a small pond. Look up at the mountainside and visualize where the gigantic slide came from. What set it off? Could it have been a massive earthquake or a top-heavy mountain? Will it happen again? At 1½ miles, reach the top of the rock dam and look down on the sparkling waters of Slide Lake. Beyond the lake is a small glacier near the top of Snowking Mountain, a small part of the glacier that carved out this valley so long ago. The dam leaks so there is no outlet stream, and the lake level fluctuates over 10 feet between a spring flood and a dry summer. The trail descends to the lake and ends abruptly. Foot-beaten paths go every which way. Pick the one that has the fewest logs to step over. To swim, you can access the water from the big boulders that make up the dam or enter the shallow water near the inlet stream. Campsites are few but choice.

Slide Lake and a shoulder of Snow King Mountain

10. Skagit River Loop

Type: Day hike
Difficulty: Easy for children
Hikable: April–November
Loop: 2 miles
High point: 500 feet
Elevation gain: minimal
Maps: Green Trails No. 48 Diablo Dam; U.S. Forest Service North Cascades National Park recreation map
Information: Marblemount Ranger District (360)873-4500

A forested loop trail west of Newhalem leads to a gravel bar under towering cliffs that rise above the Skagit River. Children will have a chance to wade in the cold water and to see sweeping views up to peaks and ridges wrapped around the town and campground. On a hot August day when I was there, a family in tennis shoes was taking turns splashing and ducking one another and then calling out, "Let's do it again."

 From I-5, take Exit 230 to North Cascades Highway 20 and pass through Sedro Woolley, Marblemount, and the Goodell Creek Campground to the Seattle City Light community of New-halem. On entering the town, immediately turn right on the road signed "Newhalem Campground" and "Visitor Center" and cross the Skagit River over a bridge incongruously regulated with red and green stoplights. Go right on Loop A and park near the amphitheater, elevation 500 feet.

Walk to the amphitheater and find the trail on the far side of the stage. In a few feet at a junction, go right and then go left at the second junction. The wide gravel-filled trail is level, lined with moss

Sword fern fronds opening up

Skagit River from Skagit River Loop Trail

and huge old cedar stumps. Children love squeezing into the cavities and playing at being elves and trolls. The trail parallels the Skagit River for a way and then in a short mile reaches the gravel bar.

For the loop, continue on. The trail makes a wide circle and returns to the campground.

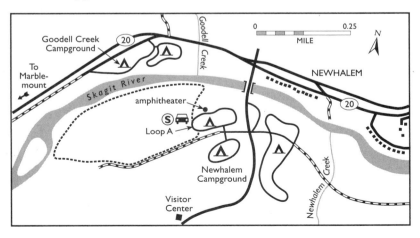

11. Stetattle Creek

Type: Day hike
Difficulty: Easy for children
Hikable: May–November
One way: ¾ mile
High point: 900 feet
Elevation gain: Minimal
Maps: Green Trails No. 48 Diablo Dam; U.S. Forest Service North Cascades National Park recreation map
Information: Marblemount Ranger District (360)873-4500

A short woodland walk along Stetattle Creek, starting on an old dike that protects the Seattle City Light town of Diablo from flooding, leads children past a series of small rapids and pools good for wading.

 Drive North Cascades Highway 20 east from Sedro Woolley, past Marblemount and Newhalem. At the intersection just before the highway crosses the Gorge Lake bridge, stay left, leaving the highway and going straight ahead on a paved road. Pass a small, free campground and cross the Stetattle Creek Bridge to find a parking area on the right side of the road opposite the trailhead, elevation 896 feet.

Begin on the shady path, skirting the backyards of houses on one side and vistas of the chattering creek on the other. In a long ¼ mile,

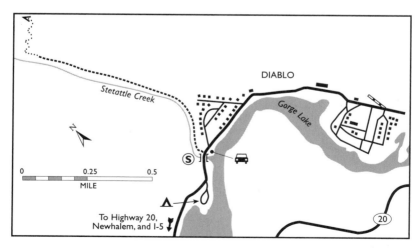

Stetattle Creek

the dike ends and the true trail starts, leading past white-water rapids next to gravel bars and deep pools with inviting beaches beside them. In several places, the path has slid away, narrowing it to a slender passage, where footing may be hazardous. If these spots have not been repaired, it may be best to turn back before reaching the deep pools at ¾ mile. The day is not lost for there are several gravel bars along the way where children can wade. At 1½ miles, fishing is allowed. The trail goes on for another mile or more.

12. Cascade Pass

Type: Day hike
Difficulty: Moderate to difficult for children
Hikable: Mid July–October
One way: 4 miles
High point: 5,392 feet
Elevation gain: 1,800 feet
Maps: Green Trails No. 80 Cascade Pass; U.S.
Forest Service North Cascades National Park
Information: Marblemount Ranger District (360)873-4500

The superb meadows and glaciered peaks of Cascade Pass are better than the best of the European Alps. The trail is graded gently enough for children, although the switchbacks gain elevation in maddeningly small increments. At the pass, in season, are myriad flower species and gasp-provoking views. Or hike it in late fall to admire the color of the vine maple and huckleberry leaves and a dusting of powdered-sugar snow on the summits.

 Drive North Cascades Highway 20 to Marblemount. Instead of turning left with the main highway, continue straight, taking the Cascade River Road across the Skagit River. Drive about 25 miles to a large parking lot at the road end, elevation 3,600 feet.

The trailhead starts switchbacking immediately. At the outset, only the bottom cliffs of Mount Johannesburg are visible, but after a mile, you can see the mountain's snowfields and hanging glaciers, which almost every summer day send avalanches thundering down. Some children find the sight and sound exciting; others may need reassurance. Still visible nearby are the waste rock and debris from a mine, which from the 1890s to the 1970s extracted no ore of value but a good deal of money from stock speculators and, in the end, a large purchase payment from the National Park Service. At about 3 miles, the trail gradually emerges from the last patches of forest and at 4 miles, it tops out at Cascade Pass, 5,392 feet.

The pass has had such heavy use that erosion has left the bench mark 2 feet above the ground surface! Camping is forbidden, to allow fragile meadows to recover. You can rest on logs and stare east down the Stehekin Valley or turn around to face the Inspiration Glacier on Eldorado Peak. Flowers climb the slopes in every direction. Clumps of subalpine fir and mountain hemlock beside the scree slopes or next to snow and rock outcrops are the only trees at this altitude, but

Eldorado Peak from Cascade Pass

below are deep green forests rolling out like magic carpets. A park ranger is frequently stationed at the pass and will identify Eldorado, Forbidden, and other peaks. Well-worn trails, excellent for older children, lead up in either of two directions: south to Mix-Up Arm and north up Sahale Arm, from which the trail dips abruptly to the deep cirque of Doubtful Lake.

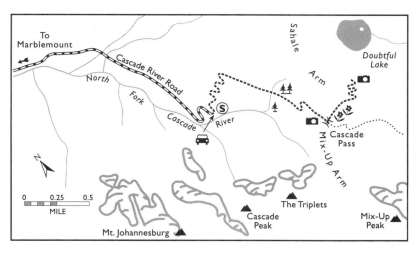

13. Lake Ann

Type: Day hike or backpack
Difficulty: Easy for children
Hikable: Mid-July–September
One way: 1¾ miles
High point: 5,475 feet
Elevation gain: 700 feet
Maps: Green Trails No. 49 Mount Logan and No. 50 Washington Pass; U.S. Forest Service Okanogan
Information: Marblemount Ranger District (360)873-4500

This short walk takes you from the highway to the high country, complete with alpine scenery. The lake might even hold a few floating icebergs!

Drive North Cascades Highway 20 east to Rainy Pass and park at the south side rest area, elevation 4,800 feet. Find the trail marked "Lakes Trails"; 10 feet along it is the one marked "Lake Ann–Maple Pass."

The hiker-only trail starts on a gentle grade through a rock slide for a scant 1 mile. At 1¼ miles is a junction; go left on the lower trail. The way narrows with roots, rocks, and marshy areas that may impede small feet but may allow their owners to inspect frogs at close range. At 1½ miles, the trail comes to Lake Ann, elevation 5,475 feet.

Small children can wade in the outlet stream, ponds, and the marsh below the lake. Even if the lake has icebergs, the possibilities for stick and stone throwing are infinite, and there's ample room to play.

Camping is not allowed near the lake, but the sites ¼ mile back are good.

On the Lake Ann Trail

Lake Ann Trail

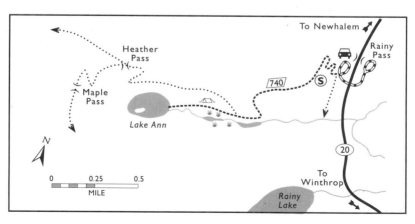

Blue Lake Trail and Liberty Bell

North Cascades Highway: East

State Route 20

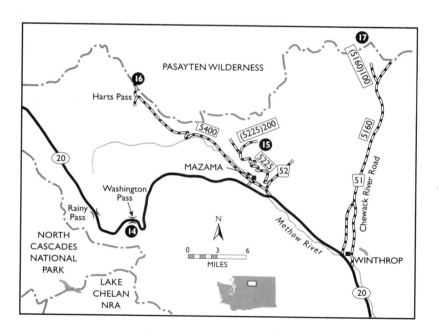

14. Blue Lake

Type: Day hike or backpack
Difficulty: Moderate for children
Hikable: Mid-July–October
One way: 2 miles
High point: 6,254 feet
Elevation gain: 1,050 feet
Maps: Green Trails: No. 50 Washington Pass; U.S. Forest Service Okanogan
Information: Methow Ranger District (509)997-2131

Many lakes have been named *Blue,* but to date this is the only one reached by a designated National Recreation Trail, a formal recognition of its outstanding beauty that does not, unfortunately, preserve it from logging or motorcycles. An abandoned old miner's cabin at the lake makes a good playhouse, and campsites are plentiful near the shoreline.

 Drive North Cascades Highway 20 for 1 mile west of Washington Pass to the Blue Lake trailhead, No. 314, elevation 5,200 feet.

Before leaving the car, gaze up at Liberty Bell Mountain. Its bell shape seems to change as the trail ascends, and it becomes more like a turreted castle. Climbers headed to Early Winter Spires share this trail before turning left for their high camp in meadows below the cliffs.

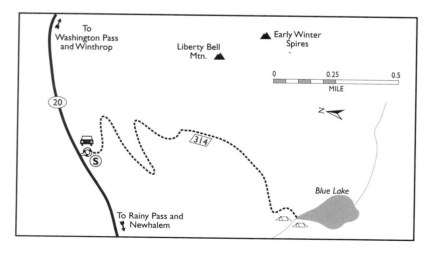

Blue Lake

Trail No. 314 is in good shape and modestly steep. At first, highway sounds follow hikers, but at ½ mile, they fade out as the path switchbacks from forest to flower-covered avalanche slope. The mix of trees shifts to subalpine firs and larches, and heather begins to appear. At 2 miles, cross the outlet stream; a few feet farther, at 6,254 feet, beautiful Blue Lake appears.

The lake is set in a deep cirque below rugged cliffs. For most of the summer, the water is kept ice cold by snow fingers beside a rock slide at the far end. Good campsites lie on both sides of the outlet stream. The old miner's cabin should not be relied upon except in direst weather.

15. Goat Peak

Type: Day hike
Difficulty: Difficult for children
Hikable: July–October
One way: 2 miles
High point: 7,000 feet
Elevation gain: 1,400 feet
Maps: Green Trails No. 51 Mazama; U.S. Forest Service Okanogan
Information: Methow Ranger District (509)997-2131

A lookout that is still occupied (in fire season) is excitement enough to make this steep and rocky trail seem less steep and rocky. From the North Cascades Highway near Early Winters, you can point it out to the children—a tiny tower perched atop the Goat Wall at the highest point on the northern horizon. Once there, they can peer down to the highway where the cars look like brightly colored ants running along a black ribbon.

The lookout was originally reached—and supplied—by a much longer trail, but the logging road has shortened the walk, and a helicopter does the supplying. The mountain goats for which the peak was named, once so abundant, were slaughtered in the 1920s. However, as hunting regulations have become more sensible, the goats are reoccupying parts of their old range. Methow Valley folks say they have, now and then, spied goats on Goat Wall.

Drive North Cascades Highway 20 to the Methow Valley. Between Early Winters and Winthrop, take the road signed "Mazama."

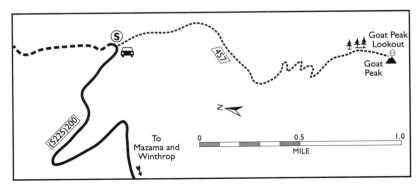

Lookout on Goat Peak with Silver Star Mountain across the Methow Valley

About 4 miles east of Mazama, go left on road No. 52 for 3.7 miles and then left on road No. 5225, signed "Goat Peak." At 8.3 miles from the county road, go right on road No. (5225)200 for another 3 miles to the trailhead, located in a saddle. The elevation is 5,600 feet.

Goat Peak trail No. 457 begins in subalpine fir and lodgepole pine, traversing a rocky ridge top, and then ascends rocky meadows. In about ½ mile, it tilts upward and steeply switchbacks to a 6,800-foot shoulder with good views. It's another half mile of easy ups and downs along the ridge top, culminating in a final steep climb, the summit, and lookout tower, at 7,000 feet.

The ridge vistas are magnificent, spreading east to farms of the Methow Valley and southwest to Silver Star, Mount Gardner, and Varden Creek, hidden by the jumble of mountains around Golden Horn. Children will enjoy talking with the lookout about how to spot fires. The lookout will be glad to have company; he or she doesn't see many fresh faces.

16. Benson Pass

Type: Day hike or backpack
Difficulty: Moderate for children
Hikable: July–October
One way: 2 miles
High point: 7,000 feet
Elevation gain: 200 feet
Maps: Green Trails No. 18 Pasayten and No. 60 Washington Pass; U.S. Forest Service Okanogan
Information: Methow Ranger District (509)997-2131

A minimum effort yields some of the most gorgeous views and flower-covered meadows in the state. The hike on the Pacific Crest Trail from Harts Pass is gentle enough for a four year old yet awe-inspiring for hikers of all ages. But be prepared for a shock. Across the valley, bulldozer tracks zigzag through beautiful alpine meadows, the work of a modern prospector operating under laws passed 120 years ago and not yet amended to fit the twentieth century.

 Drive North Cascades Highway 20 to the Methow Valley. Near Early Winters follow signs to Mazama. Turn upriver and go 20 miles on the Methow River road to Harts Pass. Turn right on the Slate Peak

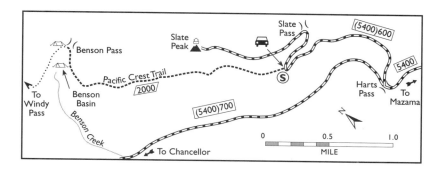

road, pass the special trailhead for horses, and at 1.5 miles, at an abrupt switchback, find a small pull-off parking area and the trailhead, elevation 6,800 feet.

The trail starts with a short climb into a meadow and then levels out and joins the Pacific Crest Trail as it contours under the summit of Slate Peak and its old lookout tower. Look out to Silver Star, the Mount Gardner massif, Azurite Peak, and Colonial Peak in the distance. Watch or hold children to make sure they don't stumble—the slope on the left, the view side, drops thousands of feet to Slate Creek. The flowers here are the envy of gardeners for their diversity and constant bloom throughout the summer season. In August, expect blue bells, shrubby cinquefoil, stone-crop, lupine, and Indian paintbrush.

At 1¾ miles, the trail contours above Benson Basin and, at 2 miles, reaches Benson Pass, elevation 6,700 feet, with views down the West Fork of the Pasayten River. There are two small campsites here, with water several hundred feet back along the trail. For better camping, drop 250 feet into Benson Basin. Practice leave-no-trace camping here, using a stove instead of a fire—the small subalpine fir and larches at 6,500 feet took a long time to grow. Windy Pass is 2 miles farther, offering different panoramas and more beauty-spot gardens—but then, so does the entire route to the Canadian Border. The kids will dream of the time they can hike *there*.

Cascade Crest Trail near Benson Pass, Mount Ballard in distance

17. Black Lake

Type:	Day hike or backpack
Difficulty:	Moderate for children
Hikable:	July–September
One way:	4½ miles
High point:	3,982 feet
Elevation gain:	800 feet
Maps:	Green Trails No. 20 Coleman Peak; U.S. Forest Service Okanogan
Information:	Methow Ranger District (509)997-2131

Black Lake is one of the gentlest trails for small children in the whole Pasayten Wilderness. Surrounded by forest, the lake is a destination with attractions for everyone—fishing, swimming, wading, birding, and just sitting and looking at mountain scenery.

Drive the Chewack River Road north from Winthrop. Upon entering the National Forest, the road becomes No. 51 and, in a few miles, No. 5160. At 20.7 miles from Winthrop, turn left on Lakes Creek road No. (5160)100 and drive 2.4 miles to the road end and trail No. 500, elevation 3,162 feet.

A very young fawn

Black Lake

The wide, level trail soon enters the Pasayten Wilderness and then follows Lake Creek through a delightful forest sprinkled with wild raspberries and blueberries that normally ripen in August. At about 1½ miles is a 10-by-20-foot boulder that rolled down from a ridge above in the winter of 1984–85, crashed through trees, bounced, and then wedged itself between four trees only a few feet from the trail. Assure the children it is unlikely to move from there.

The trail is easy the rest of the way and at 4½ miles reaches the shore of Black Lake. Children will want to wade along parts of the mile-long shore. Both ends have clean, spacious campsites, but those at the far end seem to be horse camps. All around the lake are forest-covered ridges, 7,000 feet high.

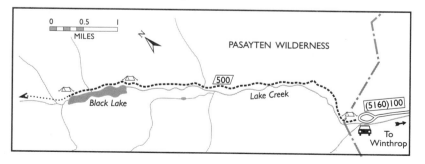

Mountain Loop Highway

State Routes 92 and 530

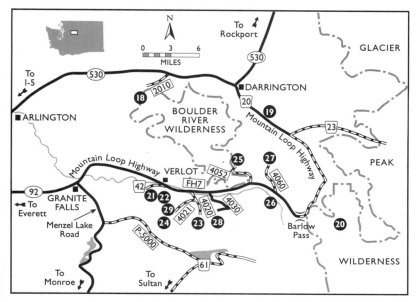

Lake Twenty-Two Trail

18. Boulder River Waterfall

Type: Day hike or backpack
Difficulty: Easy for children
Hikable: March–November
One way: 1¼ miles
High point: 1,200 feet
Elevation gain: 250 feet
Maps: Green Trails No. 77 Oso and No. 109 Granite Falls; U.S. Forest Service Mount Baker–Snoqualmie
Information: Darrington Ranger District (360)436-1155

A gentle trail, smooth and level enough for small children, takes families comfortably through old-growth forest beside a glacier-fed river in the Boulder River Wilderness. A magnificent destination is the spectacular wall-curtain waterfall at 1¼ miles. A bit beyond, an open area by the river makes a pleasant camp or lunch stop. One particular reason for preserving this valley as wilderness is that it contains one of the few remaining low-elevation old-growth forests. Foresters estimate the age of some of the trees at 750 years. All along the path are awesome old-growth Sitka spruce, silver fir, western red cedar, western hemlock, and Douglas fir. The accompanying mosses, ferns, berries, shrubs, and flowers are samples of what, before logging, all the low-elevation North Cascades valleys were like.

Drive Highway 530 east from Arlington 20 miles toward

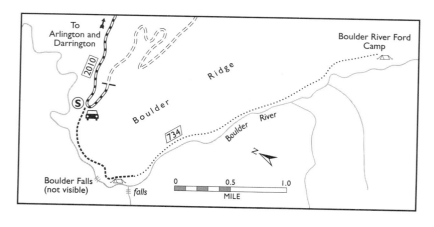

Darrington; near Milepost 41, turn right on road No. 2010, pass French Creek Campground, and at 3.6 miles from the highway, at a major switchback, find the Boulder Creek trail, elevation 950 feet.

The walk begins on the bed of an old logging railroad—wide, smooth, and well graded. The trail narrows at ½ mile and ambles through big trees shrouded with moss. At 1 mile, it passes above Boulder Falls, which lies in a canyon so deep that it can hardly be heard and is impossible to safely view. A short distance beyond, a side trail drops to the river and several campsites. The river has carved its channel so sharply that there is no floodplain, leaving the trail nowhere to go except on a narrow shelf between cliffs. At 1¼ miles, across the river, is the first of two waterfalls tumbling off cliffs into the river. By midsummer, the tumble is a quiet trickle, but thanks to the low elevation hikers can come in early spring and even winter, when higher trails are plugged up with snow.

Children enjoy hopping about in the spray and mist. This makes a fine lunch stop. The trail continues another 3 miles to Boulder River Ford and a nice campsite next to the river.

Unnamed waterfall along Boulder River

19. Old Sauk River

Type:	Day hike
Difficulty:	Easy
Hikable:	All year
One way:	3 miles, but one can turn around at any point
High point:	600 feet
Elevation gain:	None
Map:	Green Trails No. 111 Sloan Peak
Information:	Darrington Ranger District (360)436-1155

A lowland, level walk along the Sauk River bed is a Hansel and Gretel wonderland, easy enough for small children or disabled walkers, yet luminously lovely year-round. Deep forest trail skirts white water vistas and then meanders around side streams, pools, and seep ponds where in the heat of summer children can safely play. The Sauk is one of Washington's most scenic rivers, yet this trail along its banks is often overlooked as a family hike. The forest is a magical study in shades of green.

 Drive I-5 north to Exit 208 and go east on Highway 530, past Arlington to Darrington. Follow signs for the Mountain Loop Highway, which becomes road No. 20. Follow road No. 20 along the west side of the Sauk River for 3.3 miles from Darrington to the trailhead sign on the left, marked "Old Sauk Trailhead." (There is another unmarked trailhead and pullout 2 miles down the road.) Both pullouts have room for a number of cars. You may walk the trail from either end.

Begin walking through old Douglas fir, western hemlock, western red cedar, red alder, vine maple, and big leaf maple trees toward the

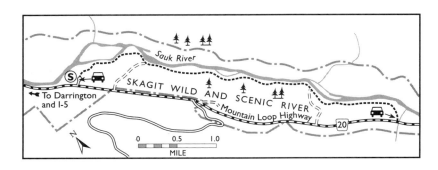

river bank. Tell children the area was logged in the early part of the century. A few remnant giant firs remain, and occasional cedar stumps with notches cut from their bases tell the story. It's not ancient forest, but the characteristics of a climax fir and hemlock forest are beginning to emerge. Mosses, probably cattail moss and goose-necked moss, encrust and festoon every tree limb and the forest floor as well in a thick carpet. In winter when tree trunks are bare, the light through the trees is filtered through the greenness. Leaning, slender, velvet-covered trunks of alder and vine maple frame views of the river, changing the outlook at every step.

The new fronds of swordfern, deer fern, and lady fern emerge from the moss in late April, along with tiny white forest flowers— foam flower, youth-on-age, a popular houseplant sold as the piggy-back plant, and vanilla leaf. Bunches of vanilla leaf were used by Indians as an insect repellent, and even after the bunches of leaves have dried, they give off a sweet vanilla scent. Native Americans called this plant *sweet after death* and used it to wrap fish. Look for glossy dark green leaves on tiny trailing vines and, in midsummer, the dainty pink and white twinflowers (*Linnaea borealis*). The blossoms rise in pairs and have a delicate fragrance. Children should know that Linnaeus, the botanist who classified all the plant kingdom, considered this flower his favorite, and it was named for him because he loved it so.

Salal

Berries children can also watch for in late summer and early autumn include red huckleberries, which like to grow in decaying cedar logs; salmonberries, with their spring scarlet flowers and summer salmon-colored fruit; and thimbleberries with white flowers and soft red berries in midsummer. On hot summer days, children can look for those overgrown bumblebees, the hummingbirds, as they fly or stand vibrating on air, inches away from red blossoms. None of the berries are dangerous, though some are better tasting than others. Low Oregon grape and salal in autumn provide dark purple berries Native Americans once made into a form of pemmican cakes. Warn children not to touch the evil-looking spines of devil's club, but in late autumn they may admire the plant's handsome red candelabra of red berries.

Old Sauk River Trail and Sauk River

Bracket fungus or "conks," wedge-shaped growths with a hard, dark, upper side and a soft, cream-colored underside, extend out horizontally from the trunks of dying Douglas firs. Children will like to discover that they can make a mark in the soft undersides of the fungus, and that the writing will remain visibly darker. Beautiful and varicolored lichens spread over the white bark of the alders. Some leathery green lichens, such as freckle pelt and lungwort, lie loose on the forest floor. Tell children they are considered delicious salad by deer and elk. A particularly spooky pale green lichen called *common witch's hair* hangs from the branches of trees like a tangled mass of wispy pale gray-green hair. Children can collect some of the strands for Halloween.

The level trail winds through the forest to provide up-close and personal views of the river. The only sound is the rush of the water

plummeting over semisubmerged rocks, splashing, rushing, and cascading. Outspreading elderly big leaf maples shade the trail from the sun's brunt until late afternoon. This trail gains very little elevation in the 3 miles it follows the Sauk River, and the tread is smooth and well maintained.

In early spring, children can look for gelatinous masses of frog eggs in puddles and backwater pools along the way. If they look closely enough, they can see tiny tadpoles moving in their sacs. The Sauk is one of the tributaries of the Skagit, which is a federally designated Wild and Scenic River. It has changed its course many times over the years and has recently eaten away its banks, so the trail has been rebuilt to accommodate this temperamental river. Children will enjoy speculating about how high it gets during flood time and how it deposits its load of logs and stumps. After the walk along the bank, children will enjoy the drive back along the lower river.

20. Goat Lake

Type: Backpack
Difficulty: Difficult for children
Hikable: June–October
One way: 5 miles
High point: 3,162 feet
Elevation gain: 1,300 feet
Maps: Green Trails No. 111 Sloan Peak; U.S.
Forest Service Mount Baker–Snoqualmie
Information: Darrington Ranger District (360)436-1155

This is an alpine lake with a history. At the turn of the century, optimistic miners built a town here, expecting to find a lode of silver— or lead, at least. Above the lake, on the cliffs of Foggy Peak, you can look for old mine shafts, easily recognized by their waste heaps and the ruins of ore-car rails leading into them. Higher still are glaciers and waterfalls tumbling down the cliffs of Foggy Peak. The trail follows the route of a wagon road used at the time of the Monte Cristo mining boom in the 1890s.

Drive the Mountain Loop Highway east from Darrington or, as described here, east from Granite Falls to the Verlot Public Service Center. From the Center go 19.5 miles to Barlow Pass and continue another 4 miles toward Darrington. About 0.2 mile beyond the Elliott

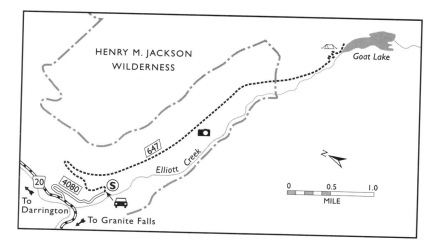

Goat Lake

Creek bridge, go right 1 mile on road No. 4080 to a large parking lot and trailhead, elevation 1,900 feet.

Old maps show the trail starting at the low end of the parking lot. Unfortunately, the trail shown on those maps is abandoned and not recommended for children. The correct way is on an abandoned road on the uphill side of the parking lot. While road walking is less fun, the trail affords views of Elliott Creek valley, Sheep Mountain, the deep gash of Pearsall Creek, and, downstream, Twin Peaks and Dickerman Mountain. At 3½ miles, the road turns into a real trail and enters the Henry M. Jackson Wilderness. At 4½ miles, four steep switchbacks ascend through old second-growth forest. In another ½ mile is the Goat Lake outlet, at 3,162 feet. Children enjoy playing and wading in this pretty lake, although the glacier-fed water is chilly.

Camping is not permitted on the shore, to allow it to recover from overuse, but picnicking is delightful. Campsites are located at the site of an old hotel on a knoll above the lake. Paying guests appreciated this spot 80 years ago, and today's families can see why.

21. Heather Lake

Type: Day hike or backpack
Difficulty: Moderate for children
Hikable: Mid-June–October
One way: 2 miles
High point: 2,400 feet
Elevation gain: 1,000 feet
Maps: Green Trails No. 109 Granite Falls; U.S. Forest Service Mount Baker–Snoqualmie
Information: Darrington Ranger District (360)436-1155

The steep and rocky trail ascends through magnificent old-growth cedar and hemlock to a lake in a cirque at the foot of Mount Pilchuck. The trail begins on a 1940s logging road, comfortably wide but surfaced with sharp rock. Children will find footing difficult in places, and toddlers may need to be carried. The last ½ mile winds through big trees. The lake is large enough for children to wade and splash in.

Drive east of Everett on U.S. 2 and follow signs to Stevens Lake. Turn left on Highway 9 and then right on Highway 92 to the town of Granite Falls. Pass through the town and turn left on the Mountain Loop Highway. Follow it to 1 mile east of the Forest Service's Verlot Public Service Center and turn right on Mount Pilchuck road No. 42. Continue 1.5 miles to the Heather Lake trailhead parking lot, elevation 1,400 feet.

Trail No. 701 begins across the road from the parking area. The trail begins in second-growth forest, and at 1 mile the beauty begins.

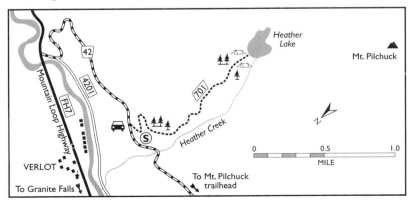

Heather Lake

The trail passes old-growth cedars and follows Heather Creek. A waterfall is a good place for a rest stop; large, flat rocks are even provided by Mother Nature.

The sounds of Heather Creek call hikers up to its source. In the next mile, six more switchbacks culminate in a puncheon bridge where the trail levels out. Begin a slight descent through open forest to a meadowy basin under the walls of Mount Pilchuck and the lake, elevation 2,400 feet.

Campsites are few, and the Forest Service permits none within 100 feet of the shore in order to let some of the mud start growing flowers again. Swimming on the south shore of the lake is a surefire delight for children. The lake is so popular that all camps are filled early on weekends; a better plan is to come on a weekday.

22. Lake Twenty-Two

Type: Day hike
Difficulty: Moderate for children
Hikable: Mid-June–October
One way: 2½ miles
High point: 2,400 feet
Elevation gain: 1,300 feet
Maps: Green Trails No. 109 Granite Falls; U.S.
Forest Service Mount Baker–Snoqualmie
Information: Darrington Ranger District (360)436-1155

The most popular trail in the Stillaguamish Valley climbs through ancient cedar trees, past picture-perfect waterfalls, and up an old rock slide overgrown with bright vine maple to a cliff-bordered subalpine lake. The lake's elevation is low enough to take children there quite early in summer or late October. The years have been hard on the trail. Between the effects of water erosion and thousands of boots, sections are nothing but roots or rough rocks that are very tough for children. The trail has some steep places but is generally gradual.

Drive the Mountain Loop Highway east from Granite Falls to the Forest Service's Verlot Public Service Center (see Hike 21). Continue east on the Mountain Loop Highway for 2 miles to a parking area on the right side, approximately 0.25 mile past the Twenty-Two Creek highway bridge, elevation 1,100 feet.

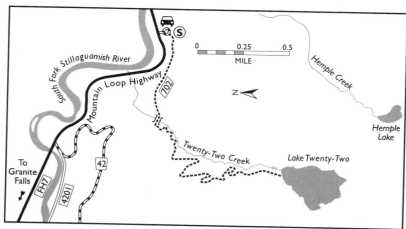

The wide trail immediately plunges into deep shade, contouring the hillside to Twenty-Two Creek, and crossing it on a "Billy Goat Gruff" bridge in ⅓ mile. Small children love looking down from the bridge to the white tumult of waterfalls.

Beyond the bridge, the trail begins a series of switchbacks, climbing steadily through old-growth forest, crossing a talus slope, and going near several exciting waterfalls. At 2¾ miles is the outlet of Lake Twenty-Two, elevation 2,400 feet.

One year, on the Fourth of July, we found it still snowed in, but that was an unusual year. Usually the only permanent snowfield is at the lake's opposite end. No camping is permitted.

Bridge and puncheon on Lake Twenty-Two Trail

23. Boardman Lake

Type: Day hike or backpack
Difficulty: Easy for children
Hikable: Mid-June–October
One way: 1 mile
High point: 2,981 feet
Elevation gain: 200 feet
Maps: Green Trails No. 110 Silverton; U.S. Forest Service Mount Baker–Snoqualmie
Information: Darrington Ranger District (360)436-1155

Two large forest lakes lie within 1 mile of the parking area. The first, Lake Evan, is just off the road—convenient for parents of toddlers who seek a wooded picnic spot. The second, Boardman Lake, with only 200 feet of trail elevation, is deeper, cleaner, and larger and offers trout fishing and views of Bald Mountain. Children will enjoy wading and splashing from the shore, whether the stay is for a day or overnight.

Drive the Mountain Loop Highway 4.5 miles east from the Forest Service's Verlot Public Service Center (see Hike 21), turn right on Schweitzer Creek road No. 4020, and continue for 5 miles, passing junctions with roads No. 4021 and No. 4024 to the trailhead, elevation 2,800 feet.

Trail No. 704 is smooth and well maintained; the path travels through gardenlike old-growth forest whose immense cedars are often

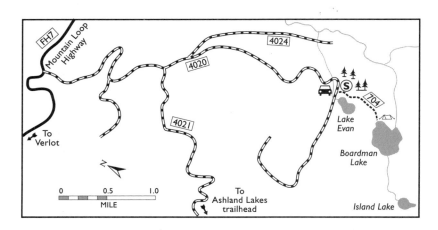

Boardman Lake

topless. These patriarchs are many centuries in the growing and
centuries in the dying, bit by bit. Lake Evan has one marshy campsite
and a backcountry toilet. Boardman Lake, elevation 2,981 feet, offers
five sites plus a group camp, each equipped with benches and fire pits.
In midsummer, children can feast on the delicious ripe huckleberries
that flourish along the shore.

24. Ashland Lakes

Type:	Day hike or backpack
Difficulty:	Moderate for children
Hikable:	July–October
One way:	1¾ miles
High point:	3,000 feet
Elevation gain:	500 feet
Maps:	Green Trails No. 110 Silverton; U.S. Forest Service Mount Baker–Snoqualmie
Information:	Darrington Ranger District (360)436-1155

A chain of three pretty woodland lakes located on Department of Natural Resources land is at the end of a rough, marshy trail. Child-delighting boardwalks encircle all of Upper Ashland and parts of Beaver Plant and Lower Ashland lakes. Campsites are at all three lakes.

Drive the Mountain Loop Highway east 4.5 miles beyond the Forest Service's Verlot Public Service Center (see Hike 21) and turn right on Schweitzer Creek road No. 4020, signed "Bear Lake" and "Bear Mountain Trail." At 2.3 miles from the highway, turn right onto Bear Lake road No. 4021. Follow this road for another 1.5 miles to the junction with the Bald Mountain–Ashland Lakes road No. (4021)016. Turn left; just past the intersection there is a gate. Park here and follow the road, now a trail, for 1 mile to the trailhead, elevation 2,500 feet.

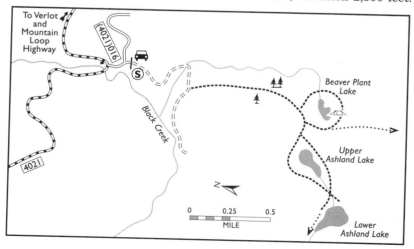

This trail has some root outcroppings larger than small children. Keep going—beautiful old-growth forest begins after ¾ mile, and it is only ½ mile more under a canopy of giant old cedars and hemlocks to Beaver Plant Lake, where there are developed campsites but no beavers. The lake is shallow and warm and has a soft mud bottom.

Continue ½ mile on a swampy trail over alternating boardwalk and log ends to Upper Ashland Lake, elevation 3,000 feet. The lake is lined with reeds, pink swamp laurel, marsh marigolds, and water lilies. You will also find rest rooms, a group camp circle at one end, and two fishing piers with benches. Wooden boardwalks will tempt most children to run and stamp their way around the small lake. In summer, the lake becomes warm enough for children to paddle, but because of its muddy bottom, they should be carefully supervised. Huckleberries in season are delicious.

For a different type of lake, drop 300 feet in ½ mile to Lower Ashland Lake. This section of trail has enough roots that toddlers will have trouble, but the deep clear lake is reason to carry them for this short distance.

Boardwalk on Ashland Lakes Trail

25. Kelcema Lake

Type: Day hike or backpack
Difficulty: Easy for children
Hikable: June–October
One way: ½ mile
High point: 3,142 feet
Elevation gain: 80 feet
Maps: Green Trails No. 110 Silverton; U.S. Forest
Service Mount Baker–Snoqualmie
Information: Darrington Ranger District (360)436-1155

This easy walk takes you through subalpine forest to a large cirque lake. Small children can happily throw stones and sticks in the water for hours or jump in for other water games. This site was once a Boy Scout camp, attained only by a trail that started way down in the valley bottom and climbed all the way in virgin forest.

 Drive the Mountain Loop Highway 14.5 miles east from the Forest Service's Verlot Public Service Center (see Hike 21). Turn left on Deer Creek road No. 4052 and continue for 4.5 miles, at one point fording a stream (on a concrete base) to the trailhead, elevation 3,100 feet.

Park and find trail No. 718, starting in a small marshy meadow.

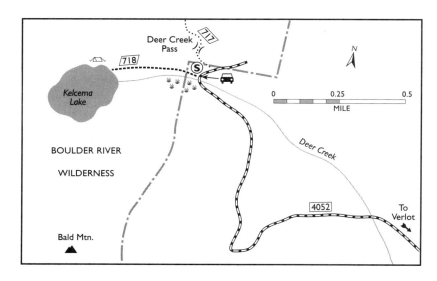

Kelcema Lake

(In June, you can see bog orchids, marsh marigolds, grass of parnassus, and chocolate bells here.) The trail enters the Boulder River Wilderness and penetrates an old forest, cresting a small knoll that overlooks the lake outfall. Part of the trail is over glacier-carved bedrock, exposed by trail builders for the width of the trail. In ½ mile is the lake, elevation 3,142 feet. Some 1,600 feet above looms Bald Mountain (a different Bald Mountain than the one seen from Boardman Lake, Hike 23).

Large campsites lie amid rock buttresses. The water, dark and deep, appears to have fish. On the north side of the lake are old and splendid Alaska cedars, many more campsites, and a backcountry toilet.

26. Big Four Ice Caves

Type: Day hike
Difficulty: Easy for children
Hikable: May–November
One way: 1 mile
High point: 1,900 feet
Elevation gain: 200 feet
Maps: Green Trails No. 110 Silverton; U.S. Forest Service Mount Baker–Snoqualmie
Information: Darrington Ranger District (360)436-1155

The nearly level trail, smooth and well maintained, crosses a series of water-spanning bridges and marsh-spanning planked walkways before arriving at the ice caves in the snowfields at the base of the 4,000-foot north face of Big Four Mountain. Hike to a stopping point beneath the tall, wide cirque headwall, dappled with snow patches and waterfalls. The ice caves are formed when the undersides of avalanche snowbanks melt from the action of water and wind. They vary in size and shape from year to year. They do not open until midsummer and are never safe to enter—ceilings have been known to collapse.

Drive the Mountain Loop Highway 15 miles east from the Forest Service's Verlot Public Service Center (see Hike 21) to the Big Four parking area, elevation 1,700 feet. The old chimney is all that remains of an inn that stood here from 1922 until it burned to the ground in 1949.

Find the plank trail crossing the marsh (it used to be a golf course!) and swamp. Older kids will have fun stamping along the planks and

Ice frequently drops from the roof of Big Four Ice Caves and boulders fall from the cliff above.

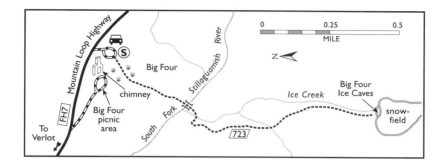

bridges. Hold tight to the hands of toddlers here. The marsh is punc- tuated with bright-yellow skunk cabbage, marsh marigolds, and such birds as kingfishers, nuthatches, and hairy woodpeckers. The gnawed branches and trees are signs that beavers are at work.

Cross the South Fork of the Stillaguamish at ½ mile and Ice Creek immediately afterward. Two benches offer welcome seats for parents packing babies. A gentle uphill through forest leads to the big picture of Big Four Mountain. The caves can be seen at the foot of a snowfield fan. If you examine the great cliff, you can spot ava- lanche chutes down which the snow slides in winter and the water falls year-round. If it's a hot day, cool off near the refrigerated caves and enjoy their unusual shapes and pale blue tones.

27. Independence Lake

Type: Day hike or backpack
Difficulty: Easy for children
Hikable: July–October
One way: ¾ mile
High point: 3,700 feet
Elevation gain: 200 feet in, 100 feet out
Maps: Green Trails No. 110 Silverton; U.S. Forest Service Mount Baker–Snoqualmie
Information: Darrington Ranger District (360)436-1155

Close enough to the road for families with small children, small enough to retain warmth from the summer sun, and large enough for several campsites, Independence Lake was named for a nearby nineteenth-century mining claim. One August, my delighted children swam all afternoon, disappointed only that we had not brought camping gear so that we could stay overnight.

Drive the Mountain Loop Highway 15 miles past the Forest Service's Verlot Public Service Center (see Hike 21) and turn left on Coal Lake road No. 4060. (Children—and drivers—may consider this a scary road because it is steep, narrow, and has a sharp drop-ff on one side, but the views of Big Four Mountain are spectacular.) Drive 4.8 miles, passing Coal Lake, to the end of the road, elevation 3,600 feet.

Trail No. 712 is a little hard to find. Look for it on the upper hillside of the parking lot. After zigzagging a few hundred yards, it enters old-growth forest and descends ¼ mile and then climbs gradually for the remaining ½ mile. Roots and rocks in the trail

may trip up very young children, but the distance is so short that

Beaver

Campsite at Independence Lake

toddlers can be carried. Watch for wild lily of the valley and salmon-berries. The trail climbs again, gradually, to reach the lake, a very deep one set beneath rock cliffs 1,000 feet tall. Independence Lake, elevation 3,700 feet, is popular with fishermen (who might object to the splashing and diving of kids). My children thought the northwest end was sunnier and best for swimming.

At least six campsites can be found if you decide to overnight here.

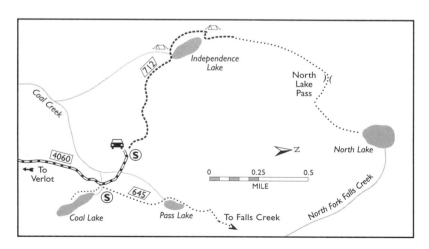

28. Cutthroat Lakes

Type: Day hike or backpack
Difficulty: Difficult for children
Hikable: July–October
One way: 4 miles
High point: 4,600 feet
Elevation gain: 1,800 feet
Map: U.S. Geological Survey Mallardy Ridge (trail not shown on any map)
Information: Darrington Ranger District (360)436-1155

These five exquisite alpine lakes are remote enough to be relatively uncrowded. Families who wish to camp can spend several days sitting and admiring the lakes' contours or wandering and exploring. The trail was built by 73-year-old Walt Bailey and his friends and has steep switchbacks and narrow tread. It is recommended for children anyway because it provides fairly direct access to the lakes.

Drive the Mountain Loop Highway past Granite Falls to the Forest Service's Verlot Public Service Center (see Hike 21). Then drive another 7 miles. Just short of the Red Bridge, turn right on Mallardy Ridge road No. 4030. At 1 mile, turn right again on road No. 4032 to the road end at 5.7 miles, elevation 3,080 feet.

The narrow trail starts out in an overgrown clear-cut and enters old-growth forest in a short distance. The way climbs steadily, steeply at times. At about 1 mile, the path drops slightly and crosses a small

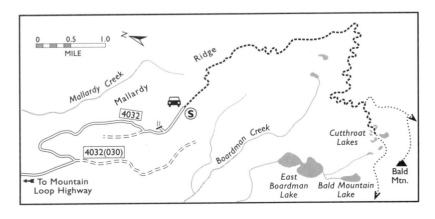

Meadows near Cutthroat Lakes

creek into meadows. This could make a satisfactory turnaround point for day hikers. Then the trail starts up again, often in marshy areas, to a 3,680-foot-high point with small glades of heather and blueberries, before dropping 200 feet to a lovely meadow at about 1¾ miles. The way continues to drop another 200 feet to pass beneath and alongside a high cliff, crosses a rock slide, and starts up.

With many berry- and heather-covered ups and downs and steep sections, the trail climbs to the first Cutthroat Lake at 4,200 feet at about 4 miles from the road. Follow the trail to the largest lake, which features a rocky island and coves and inlets to tempt swimmers and campers. The trail leads to other lakes, some with metal fire rings and campsites. The terrain is heather-covered hummocks, big subalpine trees, large white granodiorite boulders, and grassy meadows. No child will ever want to leave.

29. Bear and Pinnacle Lakes

Type: Day hike
Difficulty: Easy to Bear, moderate to Pinnacle
Hikable: June–November
One way: to Pinnacle, 2 miles
One way: to Bear, ¼ mile
High point: 3,800 feet
Elevation gain: 1,200 feet
Maps: Green Trails No. 109 and No. 110
Information: Darrington Ranger District (360)436-1155

The trail to Bear Lake is an easy ¼ mile to a forested lake with large campsites. The trail to Pinnacle Lake, on the other hand, is a steep 2 miles to a tiny subalpine tarn. The forest along the way contains many immense old-growth Alaska yellow cedars.

 On Highway 9, drive north 6 miles from Highway 2 or south 12 miles from Arlington to Highway 92 and then east to Granite Falls in 8 miles. From Granite Falls, drive east on the Mountain Loop Highway 92 past the Verlot Public Service Center. At 4.7 miles beyond it, turn right on road No. 4020 and then right again at 2.7 miles onto road No. 4021. Stay on the road to the right at an unmarked Y at 1.5 miles and continue another 1.5 miles to the trailhead, elevation 2,600 feet.

The first ½ mile of trail No. 661 has been graveled and is a beautiful walk through old-growth cedar snags. Within ¼ mile, at a

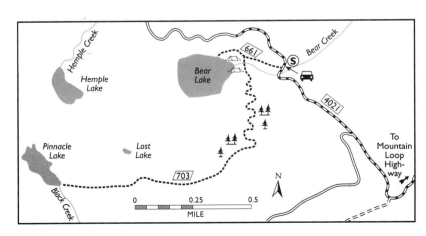

grove of old Alaska yellow and western red cedars, a fork offers two choices, one to the right to Bear Lake and the other to the left up to Pinnacle Lake.

Bear Lake has a large camping area with a possibility for a wade or swim in the shallow, muddy water. Small children will find endless possibilities for play here. Some trails around the lake suggest that fishermen find fish in its waters.

If you decide to go up to Pinnacle Lake, brace yourself for a steep muddy trek over eroded roots, marshes, and rock outcrops. The first mile leads up to a ridge. After the ridge, the second mile is less steep and breaks out into heather fields and a view down to a moss-lined pond, not Pinnacle Lake. Continue through meadows to the cliff-lined lake. Outcrops of glacier-polished rock make play areas for children. Huckleberries and alpine flower-filled meadows reward your effort. When we reached this lovely spot, the birds were singing in the rain.

Bear Lake

Ground squirrel

Stevens Pass Highway: West

U.S. 2

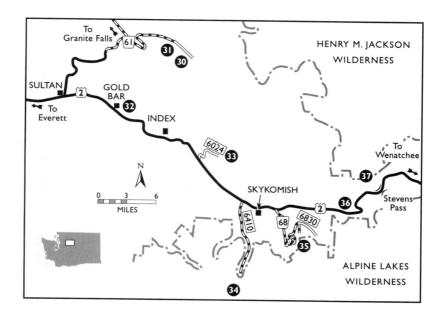

30. Boulder Lake

Type:	Day hike or backpack
Difficulty:	Difficult for children
Hikable:	July–October
One way:	4 miles
High point:	3,800 feet
Elevation gain:	2,200 feet
Maps:	Green Trails No. 142 Index; U.S. Forest Service Mount Baker–Snoqualmie

High, remote, and forested, Boulder Lake can be reached by a steep trail that starts on an old road, travels across a rock slide, and climbs up a cliff-ringed valley. The trail, one of three in the Sultan Basin tree farm, briefly follows Boulder Creek and then rejoins it at its source, the lake. Children will find the lakeshore camps and the smooth swimming beach delightful.

Boulder Lake

Drive U.S. 2 to Sultan, and at the east edge of town turn left on the Sultan Basin Recreation Area Road. At 13 miles, cross Olney Pass, enter the Spada watershed, and register as required. A short distance beyond is a three-way junction. Go straight ahead on the middle road, No. 61, for 7.5 miles. Pass numerous side roads and a boat launch; at 1 mile beyond the Greider Lakes trailhead, you'll find the Boulder Lake trailhead, elevation 1,600 feet.

The trail begins on an old logging road and in a few hundred yards crosses a wooden bridge over Boulder Creek. (If you hide a watermelon or cold drink in a pool here, it will be icy cold and waiting at the trip's end.) Road grade soon yields to the trail, built by the Department of Natural Resources in 1976. At 1 mile, the way crosses a large boulder talus and then climbs through avalanche-slope vine maple and slide alder. At about 1½ miles, it switchbacks to climb around a barrier ridge running at right angles across a cliff-walled valley. At 3 miles, the way levels out on puncheon to permit easy walking over a marsh. In the forest beyond here, the old firs and cedars are surrounded by moss. Children will be asking, "Are we almost there?" Happily, the answer is, "Yes, we are three-fourths of the way." In another mile, the trail crosses a bridge over the outlet stream to Boulder Lake, elevation 3,800 feet.

The near shore is almost all red and white heather. At the far end are cliffs, ridges, and a rock slide, colorful in fall when set off by the orange of vine maples but, because of the brush and the cliffs, you can't get there from here. You'll find six campsites, a good swimming beach, and abundant blueberries and huckleberries in season.

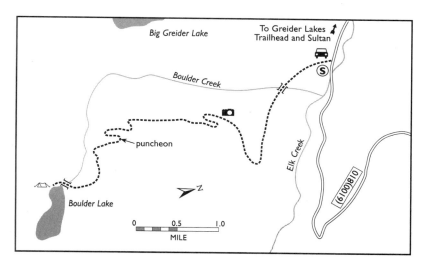

31. Greider Lakes

Type: Day hike or backpack
Difficulty: Moderate
Hikable: June–October
One way: 2 miles
High point: 2,700 feet
Elevation gain: 1,100 feet
Maps: Green Trails No. 142 Index; U.S. Geological Survey Index, Mount Stickney

Two beautiful high woodland lakes are reached at the end of a steep trail through old-growth forest. Little Greider has lily pads and is deep enough for swimming. Big Greider is deeper and is reputed to contain fine trout. Both are on Department of Natural Resources (DNR) land and offer a choice of excellent lakeshore campsites.

Drive Highway 2 east to Sultan. Just beyond the town, turn left on the Sultan Basin Recreation Area Road. At 13 miles, cross Olney Pass and enter the Spada watershed. Stop to register, as required. Greider Basin lies in the Everett watershed, where use is restricted. The entire watershed is closed to camping except by backpackers. A short distance beyond is a three-way intersection. Go straight ahead on the middle road, No. 61, for another 7.5 miles to the trailhead, elevation 1,600 feet.

The trail begins by passing a picnic area and small pond. Plan

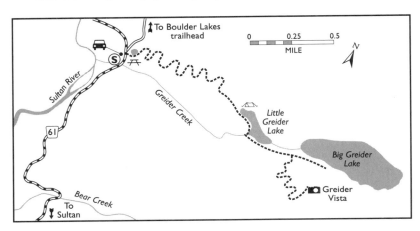

Little Greider Lake

to climb steeply up a long series of forested switchbacks. The trail has recently been repaired by DNR crews and other volunteers. Little Greider, at 2,000 feet, is long, narrow, and shallow. Lakeshore campsites are idyllic. A sturdy bridge over the Big Greider's outfall leads in ½ mile to 2,935-foot Big Greider in a narrowing valley with more campsites. The lake lies at the foot of 4,830-foot Greider Mountain, at the bottom of an enormous rock wall made up of downsloping slabs. Its lower rock slide is sometimes covered with snow to the water's edge.

Another ¾-mile trail takes hikers up to Greider Vista, with a view down the lakes and up to the surrounding peaks. While Big Greider is the more beautiful of the two lakes, swimming may be warmer in Little Greider.

32. Wallace Falls

Type: Day hike
Difficulty: Moderate for children
Hikable: April–November
One way: 2 miles
High point: 1,120 feet
Elevation gain: 880 feet
Map: Green Trails No. 142 Index

Wallace Falls is a spectacular cataract that is visible as far as the Stevens Pass highway, miles away. In recent years, it has become easily accessible. The trail is short, sometimes steep, and can be muddy

Wallace Falls

in spring and fall. However, the low elevation means it is open for
walking when the highlands are snowed in. Hazards are minimal
except at the trail's end, overlooking the falls, where spray makes
every surface slippery and requires that every child's hand be held
tight. One Mother's Day, I took two toddlers, a baby, and two grandmothers to Wallace Falls. The kids had a grand time (and were carried
much of the way), but the grandmothers never forgave me!

Drive U.S. 2 east to the town of Gold Bar. Turn left at the sign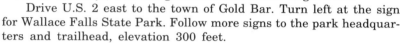
for Wallace Falls State Park. Follow more signs to the park headquar-
ters and trailhead, elevation 300 feet.

The trail starts on a service road under power lines, enters woods,
and in a long ¼ mile forks. The left fork is the Old Railroad Grade
Trail, actually a broad track. The right fork is the Woody Trail, a real
trail and the one I recommend. While the Old Railroad Grade Trail
is wide, smooth, and easy, it takes 2 miles to cover the same elevation
as the first mile of the Woody Trail.

The Woody Trail, with many ups and downs, follows near, if not
beside, the Wallace River, often going high above the stream. At 1¼
miles, the trail passes a junction with the Old Railroad Grade Trail
and then drops to a wooden bridge overlooking the North Fork of the
Wallace River, elevation 650 feet. This is a good resting point or a
picnic destination if children are young. The riverbank offers joys that
may be sufficiently satisfying.

But if the roaring of the falls cannot be resisted, climb steeply
onward in old forest. Cross a ridge into the drainage of the South Fork
of the Wallace River and climb to a shelter for the first view.

For even closer views of the thundering cataract, continue ½ mile
to the Middle Viewpoint, an ideal place to appreciate the deafening
sound of the huge volume of water. Save all commentary for later.
The falls dominate any conversation.

Finally, ½ mile above the North Fork bridge, the trail ends at
Valley Overlook, elevation 1,500 feet.

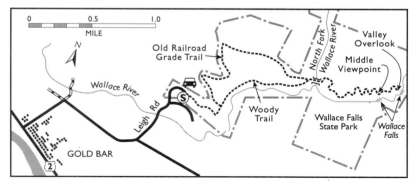

33. Barclay Lake

Type: Day hike or backpack
Difficulty: Easy for children
Hikable: June–October
One way: 1½ miles
High point: 2,442 feet
Elevation gain: 250 feet
Maps: Green Trails No. 143 Monte Cristo; U.S.
Forest Service Mount Baker–Snoqualmie
Information: Skykomish Ranger District (360)677-2414

 This shallow, low-elevation (2,442 feet) forest lake lies beneath the massive and spectacular north face of Mount Baring. Children will enjoy the chance to wade, splash, and paddle in this quiet lake, and parents will appreciate the fact that campsites are close enough to the road to make extra trips to the car if necessary. The trail is smooth and gradual, through old-growth forest.

 Drive U.S. 2 east from Everett. About 6 miles east of Index Junction, turn left at Baring on 635th Place Northeast. Cross the railroad track (the road becomes No. 6024), traverse into the valley of Barclay Creek, and 4.3 miles from the highway reach the trailhead parking area, elevation 2,200 feet.

Barclay Lake trail No. 1055 drops from the left side of the road to Barclay Creek and proceeds upstream on an easy, well-maintained trail featuring boardwalks and log ends incised like waffles or manhole covers. Cross the creek on a bridge and watch for a house-sized boulder beside the trail; the moss-covered overhang forms a magical cave. I told my children that elves and dwarves used to live here before

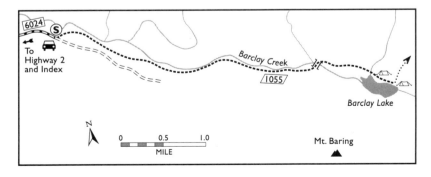

Barclay Lake beneath Mount Baring

America was discovered. It's a short distance from here to the lake.

Campsites extend along the entire north shore of the lake. The Forest Service discourages use of those within 50 feet of the lakeshore; if you decide to stay, try to cooperate.

Gazing up in open-mouthed awe at Mount Baring is enough entertainment for lots of folks. How did such a piece of landscape ever come to be? That's a long and complicated story, involving mountain building, plate tectonics, and so on. But the steepness is relatively recent and simple in origin. Of course it's a hard job convincing kids a glacier did this. ("Well, where is it then?" they ask. The answer to this is, "Gone back to Canada for more ice.") There is a sandy beach for waders and swimmers and fishing for everyone. Expect weekends to be crowded.

34. Lake Dorothy

Type: Day hike or backpack
Difficulty: Moderate for children
Hikable: June–October
One way: 2 miles
High point: 3,058 feet
Elevation gain: 858 feet
Maps: Green Trails No. 175 Skykomish; U.S. Forest Service Mount Baker–Snoqualmie
Information: Skykomish Ranger District (360)677-2414
Wilderness permit required

The short, very popular, and much-used trail along the rushing Miller River leads quite quickly to one of the largest forest lakes in the Alpine Lakes Wilderness. Opportunities for water activities are abundant. The track is so eroded that exposed roots and rocks make travel difficult for short legs. However, only the last ½ mile is steep, climbing to the source of the Miller, lovely Lake Dorothy.

Drive U.S. 2 east from Everett toward Stevens Pass. Approximately 11 miles east of Index Junction (3.5 miles short of Skykomish, just before the tunnel), go right on the Old Cascade Highway through Money Creek Campground. At 1.2 miles, take Miller River road No. 6410 and drive to its end.

This trail, which was damaged by flooding in 1995, has been repaired since by volunteers from the Washington Trails Association. It starts in big old cedars and firs. Boggy spots are lighted in spring by torchlike skunk cabbage. At 1¼ miles, the trail crosses Camp Robber Creek on a bridge that is in its own right a sufficient destination.

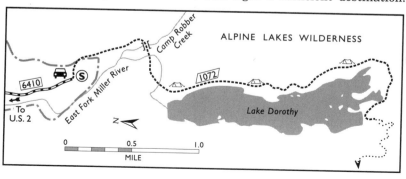

Children can spend a lunch hour stomping back and forth on the bridge to see if their stomps can compete with the waterfall's roar. If they do not recognize John Muir's favorite bird, the water ouzel, tell them to watch for a gray bird skittering along the surface of the water, pausing now and then to perch on a rock, dip-dip-dipping at the knees.

Actually, after Camp Robber Creek, the final bit of trail to the lake and its outlet logjam, at 3,058 feet, are an anticlimax.

The trail continues along the lakeshore to the head, with choice campsites for families arriving early on weekends or midweek. Rocky cliffs rise high on the opposite shore.

Please note: A bridge washout on the road in 1996 added 2¼ miles to the trail distance. Check with the ranger before starting out.

Camp Robber Creek bridge on Lake Dorothy Trail

35. Tonga Ridge

Type: Day hike
Difficulty: Easy for children
Hikable: July–October
One way: 3 miles
High point: 4,900 feet
Elevation gain: 500 feet
Maps: Green Trails No. 176 Stevens Pass and No. 175 Skykomish; U.S. Forest Service Mount Baker–Snoqualmie
Information: Skykomish Ranger District (360)677-2414
Wilderness permit required

A trail gradual enough to stroll with small children climbs easily to meadowlands, with views of Glacier Peak and the Central Cascades. In fall, there are huckleberries to pick; on early summer mornings, children can watch for deer.

 Drive U.S. 2 east 1.8 miles past Skykomish and go right on Foss River road No. 68. At 2.5 miles, turn left on road No. 6830, go another 7 miles, and then turn right on road No. (6830)310. Go 1.5 miles to its end at a parking lot, elevation 4,400 feet.

The road ends virtually at timberline, amid spectacular views of Index, Persis, Baring, and Glacier Peak. Why leave the car at all? Because the meadows beckon. Begin on an old fire trail ascending

Mule deer

Tonga Ridge near Sawyer Pass

modestly through a forest of mixed conifers. In 1 mile, the trail breaks
out of the forest into broad meadows. The view south to the craggy
peaks along the Cascade crest is superb. The trail now follows the
crest through meadows of huckleberry and heather.

   The views cannot improve—they just change from one gorgeous
vista to another. At 3 miles, you'll find sometimes watered and sometimes dry campsites at Sawyer Pass, 4,800 feet. Enjoy this hike in
late September for spectacular fall color and blueberries.

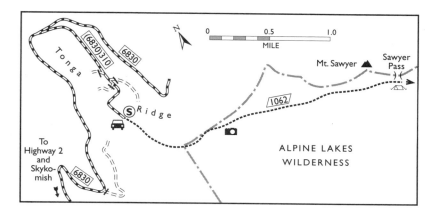

36. Stevens Pass Lakes

Type: Day hike or backpack
Difficulty: Moderate for children
Hikable: July–October
One way: to Skyline Lake, 1½ miles
One way: to Grace Lakes, 1¾ miles
High point: 5,092 feet and 4,850 feet
Elevation gain: 900 feet and 750 feet
Maps: Green Trails No. 176 Stevens Pass and No. 144 Benchmark Mountain; U.S. Forest Service Mount Baker–Snoqualmie
Information: Skykomish Ranger District (360)677-2414

On each side of Stevens Pass, high above on ridges, are delightful little lakes—Grace Lakes on the south and Skyline Lake to the north. All are ringed by meadows of heather and blueberries. The lakes are shallow; some may even dry up in late summer, but when full and warm, they make ideal family camps. Unfortunately, reaching any of the lakes requires a hike up steep service roads that can be hot in the noon sun.

Drive U.S. 2 to the summit of Stevens Pass, elevation 4,056 feet. The amazingly remote Skyline Lake is only 1.5 miles above the summit. The trail is a steep road suitable for jeeps and 4x4s.

Walk or drive ¼ mile up the paved driveway past a number of vacation cabins to a small parking space. Here the road becomes a

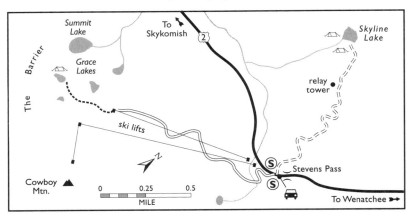

Skyline Lake

jeep track and turns uphill with a vengeance—at as much as an 18 percent grade, possible for pedestrians but too rugged for all but a few 4x4s. With every step upward, the views of the ski area and surrounding ridges widen. The blueberries here are renowned; commercial pickers spend much of the late summer here, but they don't get them all. Here is another source of energy food for kids. At 1 mile, the trail passes a relay tower in a large clearing and in a steep ½ mile more reaches the lakeshore. Camping here is at the end of the jeep track and across from the outlet. One Labor Day, I saw large bear tracks on the shoreline; I hope he enjoyed the juicy blueberries as much as I did.

For Grace Lakes, park on the south side of the pass near the ski area. On the west side of the parking lot, find a gated service road. Walk past numerous ski area buildings and, with a slight dip, pass directly under chairlifts. Stay left at the first junction and right at the next. Pass under the red chairlift (Barrier Ski Lift) and climb an ever-steepening rocky road to the top terminal of the turquoise Brooks Lift, at 4,850 feet. Here the road gives way to a boot-beaten path through heather, blueberries, and mountain ash. From here, it is ¼ mile to campsites at the largest of the four shallow, spring-fed Grace Lakes.

For exploration, use the USGS map to reach the other two accessible lakes. The lowest of the Grace Lakes does not have a trail. Summit Lake, the largest and deepest in the Stevens Pass area, is only ½ mile farther, but it is not recommended for children due to the poor condition of the trail.

37. Lake Valhalla

Type: Day hike or backpack
Difficulty: Moderate for children
Hikable: July–September
One way: 5½ miles
High point: 5,050 feet
Elevation gain: 1,100 feet in, 200 feet out
Maps: Green Trails No. 144 Benchmark Mountain and No. 176 Stevens Pass; U.S. Forest Service Wenatchee
Information: Lake Wenatchee Ranger District (509)763-3103

Lake Valhalla is named for the Teutonic home of the gods for good reasons—the heather meadows, the rock slides, the ridges and cliffs of Lichtenberg Mountain. It is the first in a series of lakes north of Stevens Pass on the Pacific Crest Trail. Children will love its fairy-tale charm. Mine told me they thought trolls would live in such a place.

 Drive U.S. 2 to the summit of Stevens Pass and park on the north side of the summit area at the east end, elevation 4,056 feet. Join the Pacific Crest Trail behind the garage and a power station.

The first 1½ miles, almost level, lie on the original grade of the Great Northern Railroad, constructed over the top of the pass in 1893. The grade was abandoned when the Cascade Tunnel was built in the aftermath of the Wellington Avalanche of 1910, which swept away part of that town and two train cars of people, killing ninety-six. Now it is part of the Pacific Crest Trail.

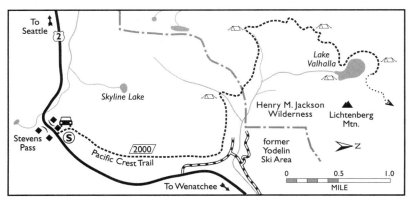

Lake Valhalla

Along the early part of the hike, look down to the former Yodelin ski area and cabins, which in 1971 were also struck by a series of avalanches. (The avalanches had been occurring almost every winter but were never noticed until the developer built in their path.) Views east are down Stevens Creek to Nason Creek and the Stevens Pass Highway. At 1½ miles, the trail rounds a ridge, crosses a little stream, and enters the Henry M. Jackson Wilderness. The trail is generally well graded and reasonably smooth.

At 2½ miles and at 3 miles are small streamside campsites. At 3½ miles are a meadowy basin and a marsh, where children can pause to do some splashing. Camping is possible here though not really ideal. A bit farther on, at just under 4 miles, are numerous campsites next to a large meadow. Any one of these campsites would make a good turnaround point for younger children.

The trail climbs to another meadow, elevation 5,030 feet, and then drops steeply to the shores of Valhalla at 4,830 feet, the source of Nason Creek.

Campsites are located at the outlet, with the most numerous and easiest to reach at the upper end. All are popular, so plan to leave home early to get a good spot.

Lake Valhalla

Stevens Pass Highway: East

U.S. 2 and U.S. 97

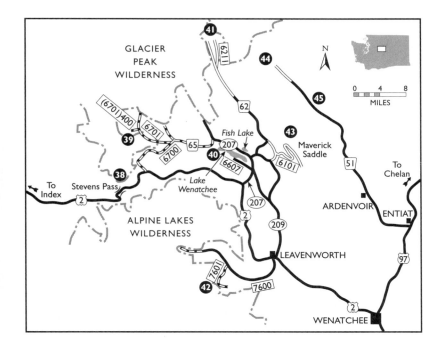

38. Lake Janus

Type: Day hike or backpack
Difficulty: Moderate for children
Hikable: Mid-July–October
One way: 3½ miles
High point: 4,680 feet
Elevation gain: 1,100 feet in, 700 feet out
Maps: Green Trails No. 144 Benchmark Mountain;
U.S. Forest Service Wenatchee
Information: Lake Wenatchee Ranger District (509)763-3103

The Roman god Janus had two faces so he could see in two directions at once. A traveler on this trail through the Henry M. Jackson Wilderness can look toward both eastern and western Washington while walking the ridge that separates them—the Cascade Crest. Lake Janus, a beauty, is set among alpine meadows at the base of 6,007-foot Jove Peak. Adults will enjoy the scenery along the way; children can play in the lake. The trail has some steep portions but is smooth and well maintained. Note that there is a 700-foot descent; it must be climbed on the return.

 Drive U.S. 2 east from Stevens Pass for 4.5 miles, and turn left on the Smith Brook road No. 6700. Cross Nason Creek bridge, turn left, and follow the road to the Smith Brook trailhead, elevation 3,800 feet. Parking near the trailhead is difficult, so many hikers park 0.25 mile below the last switchback and walk to the trailhead.

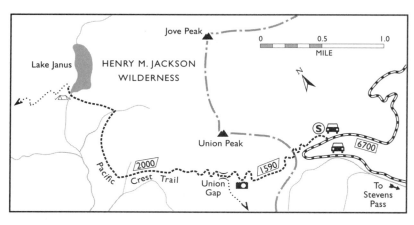

Trail No. 1590 switchbacks steeply up to Union Gap, elevation 4,680 feet, and a junction with the gentler grade of the Pacific Crest Trail. Views east are toward forests of larch, shimmering aspen, and pines along Nason Creek. The views west are dark with Douglas fir, hemlock, and cedar.

At Union Gap, go right, following the Pacific Crest Trail northward, losing 700 feet to pass under cliffs of Union Peak. From this low point, the trail climbs again to the shores of Lake Janus, elevation 4,146 feet, 3½ miles from the road.

Camping here is good but crowded by Pacific Crest Trail traffic. The water is clear, deep, and cold; children will find it better for skipping stones than for bathing. If you decide to stay, bring a stove—fuel wood is scarce and fires are prohibited.

Lake Janus

39. Heather Lake

Type: Day hike or backpack
Difficulty: Difficult for children
Hikable: July–October
One way: 3¼ miles
High point: 3,953 feet
Elevation gain: 1,300 feet.
Maps: Green Trails No. 144 Benchmark Mountain;
U.S. Forest Service Wenatchee
Information: Lake Wenatchee Ranger District (509)763-3103

The trail is steep; the lake is big and beautiful. The hot summer day when I was there, children were having a fine time swimming and playing on the rocks around the shore.

 There are two ways to the Heather Lake trailhead. From Stevens Pass, drive 4.5 miles east on U.S. 2, turn left on Smith Brook road No. 6700, and go over Rainy Pass; you continue many more miles over a gravel road to its end at the Heather Lake trailhead. Or, from the north end of Lake Wenatchee, go left on the Little Wenatchee River road No. 65 and then left on road No. 6700 and cross the Little Wenatchee River to a junction with the Smith Brook Road. Go straight ahead on road No. 6701 for 4.7 miles, turn left on road No. (6701)400, and go another 2.3 miles to the road end and trailhead, elevation 2,600 feet.

The trail begins in old-growth forest in unprotected Wenatchee

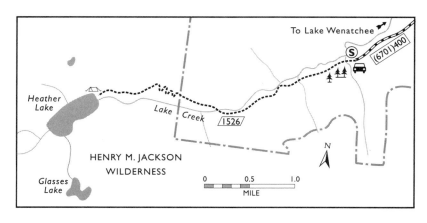

Heather Lake

National Forest. At 1 mile, it crosses Lake Creek and enters the Henry
M. Jackson Wilderness. At 1½ miles, a series of murderously steep
switchbacks climbs 900 feet in a very long mile that will seem like
ten. (I went by two boys trying to lug an inflated raft up the trail.
I wonder if they made it—the last I saw of them they were complain-
ing that there was no place to set it down.) The grade finally eases
and continues another ¾ mile to sparkling Heather Lake, elevation
3,953 feet, in a glacier-scooped cirque basin beneath Grizzly Peak.
Many good campsites are scattered about among berry bushes and
driftwood. Each comes with a view.

40. Hidden Lake

Type: Day hike or backpack
Difficulty: Easy for children
Hikable: May–November
One way: ½ mile
High point: 2,300 feet
Elevation gain: 300 feet
Maps: Green Trails No. 145 Wenatchee Lake; U.S. Forest Service Wenatchee
Information: Lake Wenatchee Ranger District (509)763-3103

Hidden Lake lies unseen scarcely a half mile above huge Lake Wenatchee. Many families will prefer Hidden Lake, away from the crowds at Lake Wenatchee State Park, for its ponderosa-pine setting and that special feeling only a mountain lake that is located away from a road can provide. One sunny afternoon, I watched many parents with toddlers and babies playing at the water's edge.

From U.S. 2 between Stevens Pass and Leavenworth, turn north on Highway 207 toward Lake Wenatchee. At 4 miles, turn left to Lake Wenatchee State Park. In a short distance (before the park boundary), turn left again on road No. 6607. Drive 5 miles to Glacier View Campground and trailhead, elevation 2,000 feet.

So heavily used that its bony rocks and roots are showing, trail No. 1510 is ½ mile of steep switchbacks through dry underbrush. Lost on the way is the racket of powerboats on Lake Wenatchee.

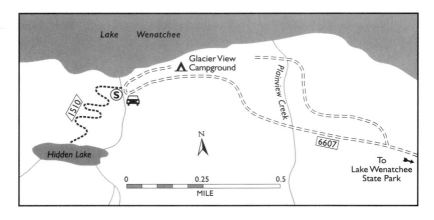

Hidden Lake

Hidden Lake, elevation 2,500 feet, is long and narrow and wraps itself around the base of Nason Ridge. Families, fishermen, and bathers floating in rafts for the joy of floating have a wonderful time in its cool waters.

41. Spider Meadow

Type: Day hike or backpack
Difficulty: Moderate to difficult for children
Hikable: July–October
One way: 5 miles
High point: 5,500 feet
Elevation gain: 2,000 feet
Maps: Green Trails No. 113 Holden; U.S. Forest
Service Wenatchee
Information: Lake Wenatchee Ranger District (509)763-3103

Beneath a spectacular headwall of cliffs and waterfalls sprawls a marvelous wide meadow valley, the reward for a 5-mile walk into the Glacier Peak Wilderness. Camping is amid flower fields, beside a cold meandering stream. The deer here are almost tame.

Drive U.S. 2 east 17 miles from Stevens Pass and turn north on the Lake Wenatchee Road. Pass Wenatchee State Park and cross the Wenatchee River. Turn right at the final junction, go 1.5 miles, and then turn left on Chiwawa River road No. 62, signed "Trinity." Drive 22 miles, turn right on road No. 6211, signed "Phelps Creek," and go 2 miles to a gate and the trailhead, elevation 3,500 feet.

The hike begins on a gated miners' road, passing the Carne Mountain trail at ¼ mile, Box Creek at 1 mile, and Chipmunk Creek at 1¾ miles, a good turnaround close to Phelps Creek. At 2⅔ miles, where the road becomes trail, enter the Glacier Peak Wilderness. At 3½ miles, cross Leroy Creek and pass the Leroy Creek trail.

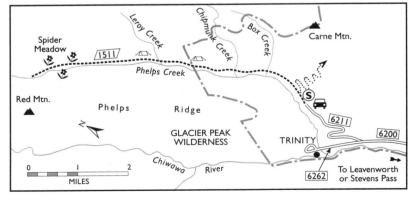

All of the creeks are delightful resting places—and campsites, if necessary. From Leroy Creek, it's an easy 1½ miles through spruce, noble fir, and alpine flowers or berries in season to Spider Meadow, elevation 5,500 feet.

The parkland extends more than a mile north and south, bordered upvalley by the cliffs of Dumbbell and Red mountains. Campsites edge the meadow; walk to the upper end for more secluded campsites at the base of a talus slope and to see the ruins of an old miner's cabin. In early morning or evening, children may expect to see the curious deer approach camp and play, chasing each other through the flowers.

Flower-covered Spider Meadow

42. Eightmile Lake

Type: Day hike or backpack
Difficulty: Difficult for children
Hikable: May–November
One way: 3½ miles
High point: 4,461 feet
Elevation gain: 1,500 feet
Maps: Green Trails No. 177 Chiwaukam Mountains; U.S. Forest Service Wenatchee
Information: Leavenworth Ranger District (509)762-1413
Wilderness permit required

The Icicle River Valley burned in the summer of 1994. At least one-third of the trees along this trail—ponderosa pine, hemlocks, and cedars—were transformed into charred sentinels and silver forest. New life is generating, however, as it always has. Children will enjoy seeing the vestiges of old stumps surrounded by green growth and hearing the story of searing crown fires roaring up Eightmile Creek. The lake is still a lovely glacier-carved irrigation reservoir with a dam at one end. Poignantly, signs requesting that no campfires be built near the shoreline are posted on burned trees along the shoreline, and the air still smells of fire.

     Take U.S. 2 to Leavenworth. On the west side of town, turn right on Icicle Creek Road and drive 8.5 miles. Turn left on Eightmile Creek road No. 7601 and drive 3 miles to Eightmile Creek trail No. 1552, elevation 2,900 feet. Be sure to fill out a Wilderness Permit.

Begin with a steep ½ mile ascent through partially burned trees,

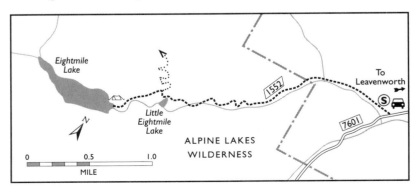

Eightmile Lake

wild roses, and fireweed. The next ½ mile on an old logging roadbed will be easier before you turn into a grove of scorched and scarred old-growth trees alongside the white water of Eightmile Creek in the Alpine Lakes Wilderness. This would make a good resting place or turnaround point.

At 2½ miles, you start upward again. Look for places along the needle-carpeted trail where the stumps burned so hot into the ground that the roots left holes shaped like octopus tentacles. Climbing steadily, at 3 miles the trail comes to a small lake that fluctuates according to water needs below. Continue up another ½ mile through a massive red rock slide. The reward for your 3¼ miles is Eightmile Lake, elevation 4,461 feet.

Look for the vintage 1930s hand-built stone dam and its ruined, rusty petcock. Swimming here, amid glacier-carved rocks and driftwood logs, can be refreshing—that is to say, cold—but after the hot trail, good . . . very good. Campsites are on the shoreline to the right.

43. Mad River Vacation

Type: Backpack
Difficulty: Moderate for children
Hikable: Mid-July–October
One way: To campsites 2½, 3½, and 6 miles
Loop trip: 12 miles
High point: 6,400 feet
Elevation gain: 1,250 feet
Maps: Green Trails No. 146 Plain; U.S. Forest Service Wenatchee
Information: Lake Wenatchee Ranger District (509)763-3103

Here is a glorious place to take children for 3 days or a week. You'll find streams to wade in, a lake to swim in, loop trips, and viewpoints—all on a plateau where the subalpine forest is richly filled with alpine meadows.

The area is seldom used by hikers because it is open to motorcyclists. But midweek, wheels are scarce. Then a family can have miles of wild area to itself. Even on weekends, machine riders go home by nightfall. There are countless campsites to choose from; pick the one that suits your pleasure and your speed.

From U.S. 2 between Stevens Pass and Leavenworth, turn north on Highway 207 toward Lake Wenatchee State Park. Pass the park and, at 4 miles from U.S. 2, just past the Wenatchee River bridge, go straight ahead on paved county road No. 22. Continue on this road,

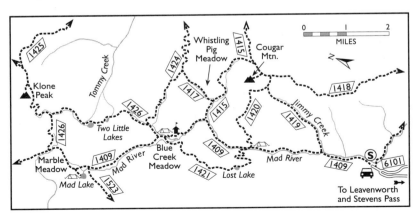

Mad River Trail

dodging side roads to Fish Lake and also the new Chiwawa River road. At 1.5 miles from U.S. 2, cross the Chiwawa River in the middle of a vacation-home development. Turn north on the Chiwawa River road No. 16 for 1.6 miles and turn right on road No. 6101. At 7.3 miles from the county road, after a final steep and narrow 2 miles, find Maverick Saddle. An even rougher road, probably best walked, leads 0.3 mile to the trailhead, signed "Mad River Trail 1409," elevation 4,250 feet.

The first mile of trail has few steep ups and downs. A sturdy bridge spans the Mad River, which is not much of a river here near the headwaters but a splendid creek. At 2½ miles is the first of many attractive streamside campsites; here you can adjust your ambitions to the capabilities of your children. At 4 miles, cross the river on a driftwood log and, at 4½ miles, recross on boulders. At 5 miles, enter the first of the meadows and, at 6 miles, reach unmanned Blue Creek Camp Guard Station, built in the 1920s—an ideal place for a base camp, elevation 6,100 feet.

Day trips abound. Hike 2 miles to Mad Lake on a fairly level trail through meadows and subalpine forest; swimming is good on a small beach at the inlet. Hike to Two Little Lakes at 2½ miles; or loop through Whistling Pig Meadow, named for its colony of marmots. A more strenuous hike is to the top of Cougar Mountain for panoramic views of forest and mountains. The map will suggest other loops.

Half of the motorcycle drivers on these trails are courteous and will slow down when passing; the other half, mainly unsupervised young- sters, whiz by at full speed, using hikers as part of an obstacle course.

44. Myrtle Lake

Type: Day hike or backpack
Difficulty: Moderate for children
Hikable: May–November
One way: 4 miles
High point: 3,765 feet
Elevation gain: 600 feet
Maps: Green Trails No. 114 Lucerne; U.S. Forest Service Wenatchee
Information: Entiat Ranger District (509)784-1511

Along the road beyond Ardenvoir enjoy the pageant of forest regrowth since the great Entiat Fire of 1966. This is the way nature has been restoring itself after disasters for thousands of years. Then hike a gently graded trail along the Entiat River to a peaceful forest lake. In May and June, expect to see deer with fawns along the way. The forested trail is within sound of the Entiat River but in sight of the water only twice. Children may find the trail a bit boring, but they will love the blue-green lake, which lies under tall cliffs.

From Entiat on U.S. 97, drive the Entiat River road 38 miles to its end, elevation 3,100 feet, and find the trailhead for Entiat River trail No. 1400 at the upper end of the parking lot.

Hikers share the way with horses, bicycles, and the occasional motorcyclist, all creating a busy and dusty trail. The gradual trail passes through a varied forest of lodgepole pine, fir, and cottonwood. At 3 miles, cross Anthem Creek, where there are a number of campsites, the best of which are 300 feet downstream from the bridge. In a short 4 miles, turn left on the Cow Creek Meadow trail No. 1404, heading for Myrtle Lake. If intending to camp, bear left for

Myrtle Lake

Myrtle Lake

a short distance, climbing another 100 feet to the lake. If hiking for the day, stay on the main trail and make the rather messy crossing of the lake's outlet to reach a nice waterside meadow.

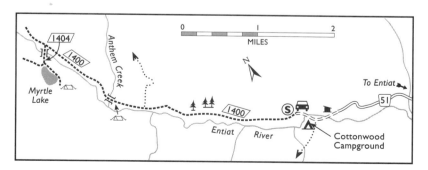

45. Silver Falls

Type: Day hike
Difficulty: Moderate for children
Hikable: June–November
Loop: 1 mile
High point: 3,000 feet
Elevation gain: 600 feet
Maps: Green Trails No. 146 Plain; U.S. Forest Service Wenatchee recreation map
Information: Entiat Ranger District (509)784-1511

A loop trip past beautiful rapids, climbing over the top of fan-shaped Silver Falls, offers a chance to look through a curtain of water. Along the way up the Silver Creek loop trail are small waterfalls. Mist and spray will cool children (and their parents) on a hot day.

Drive east on Stevens Pass Highway 2 to the west side of Wenatchee. Stay on Highway 2 as it curves under itself and pick up Highway 97, signed "Lake Chelan." Follow Highway 97 to just short of the town of Entiat and go left on the Entiat River road 29 miles to a large parking area next to the entrance to the Silver Falls Campground, across the road from the Silver Falls trailhead, elevation 2,400 feet.

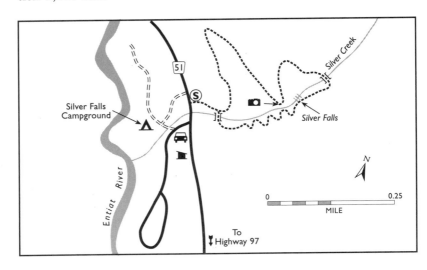

The trail is steep and paved with many giant stone steps. In a few hundred feet, you will have a choice of following the creek up its left or right side. Cross the creek on a bridge with unique curved railings. The right side switchbacks up beside the tumbling creek, close enough at times that you can feel the spray. At approximately ⅔ mile, a short side trail takes you to the bottom of the falls. If, in midsummer, the rocks are dry behind the falls, it is possible to walk behind them into a small cave and look out through the pouring water. A child of any age will enjoy this treat.

The trail then climbs over the top of the falls, crosses the creek, and heads down to a dramatic viewpoint. Then it makes a long switchback away from the creek before completing the loop.

Silver Falls

Snoqualmie Pass Highway: West

Interstate 90

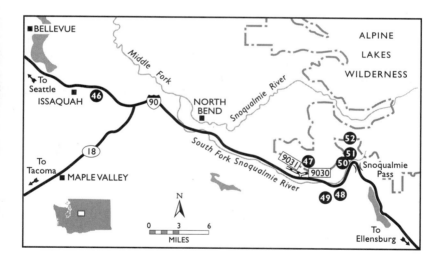

Denny Creek

46. High Point Trailhead

Type: Day hike
Difficulty: Moderate to difficult
Hikable: Most of the year
One way: to Talus Rocks, 1¼ miles
One way: to West Tiger Vista, 2½ miles
Elevation gain: 600 feet and 1,800 feet
High point: 2,000 feet
Map: Check trailhead reader board

With three trail opportunities, High Point trailhead is ideal for children. Choose between the easy Tradition Lake trail, a moderate climb to Talus Rocks where children can find out about the bat caves, and a very strenuous climb to the top of West Tiger Vista 3 for a view over Seattle to the Olympic Mountains and south to Mount Rainier, giving children the right to boast they climbed a real mountain. The trick is to pick the hike that will give your children a challenge without discouraging them from hiking. Only you will know which is best.

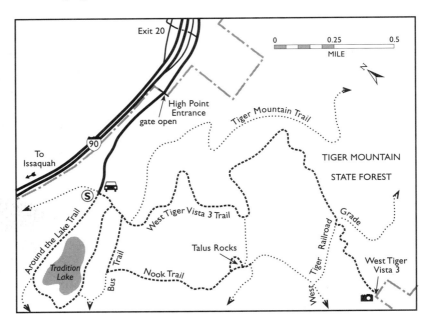

Experienced hikers use Tiger Mountain trails in the winter and spring when the Cascade Mountain trails are buried under snow. The trails are especially good in the middle of April when alders are budding, trilliums and bleeding heart are in bloom, and the sword ferns are unfurling their fronds, which resemble elephants' trunks.

Drive I-90 east of Issaquah to Exit 20, which is signed "High Point." Go right and right again and drive the frontage road a short 1 mile to the trailhead parking area. The parking lot holds only 85 of the 150 cars found there on a sunny weekend, so arrive early.

For Talus Rocks, follow the West Tiger Vista 3 Trail about 500 feet and go right on Bus Trail a short 1,000 feet and then left on Nook Trail for a long mile. The way starts out easy but gets progressively steeper. At about 1½ miles, reach the boulders. A circular trail squeezes through a narrow passage and passes a deep hole, the overhangs, and the fenced-off Bat Cave. Bats are nocturnal, so they are seldom seen, but they contribute to our well-being by consuming vast numbers of harmful and pesky flying insects, including mosquitoes, every night.

West Tiger Vista 3 Trail is a very steep trail for children, climbing 800 feet a mile, but if your children are up to it, they will be rewarded by reaching a summit. From the parking area, follow the West Tiger Vista 3 Trail passing Bus Trail on the right, Tiger Mountain trail on the left, and in about ¾ mile, Connector Trail (not recommended for children). At 2 miles, cross the West Tiger Railroad Grade where the trees become shorter and windswept. At 2½ miles, arrive at the bald summit and rewarding views and a well-deserved rest.

Gate protecting Bat Cave

47. Talapus Lake

Type: Day hike or backpack
Difficulty: Moderate for children
Hikable: July–October
One way: 2 miles
High point: 3,450 feet
Elevation gain: 1,120 feet
Maps: Green Trails No. 206 Bandera; U.S. Forest Service Mount Baker–Snoqualmie
Information: North Bend Ranger District (360)888-1421
Wilderness permit required

Easy access, a short trail, camping, fishing, and proximity to other woodland lakes are the reasons Talapus is one of the most popular lakes in the greater Snoqualmie Pass area. The trail continues on from Talapus to Olallie and numerous other lowland lakes.

Drive I-90 east of North Bend approximately 15 miles to Bandera

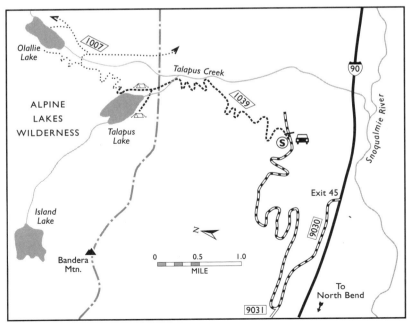

Talapus Lake

Exit 45. Take the overpass to the north side of the highway and follow road No. 9030. At 0.25 mile is a junction with road No. 9031; turn right and remain on road No. 9030 for 3 miles. Find the trailhead at the end of the road, elevation 2,600 feet.

Trail No. 1039 begins in a former clear-cut with deciduous undergrowth over an old roadbed. The trail climbs gradually in long switchbacks, narrowing as it enters second growth. At 1 mile, you come close to a stream with large rocks for resting on. Some can serve as picnic tables if this is your lunch stop.

At 1¾ miles, the trail levels and enters the Alpine Lakes Wilderness, where you will see enormous old-growth cedars. Watch for wild lily of the valley and the tiny pink bells of twinflower lining the trail. The Swedish botanist Linnaeus, who classified the plant kingdom into genera and species, chose twinflower over all others in the world to bear his name—*Linnaea.*

The trail follows the lake's outlet stream, zigzagging toward and away from it. Some of the zags also make good resting places. Just before the lake, there is a fork, with the right trail offering more campsites but the left has some good ones as well. At 2 miles comes the first view of the lake, set in a deeply wooded basin, elevation 3,680 feet. There are at least fifteen campsites for the 4,000 or more visitors a year this lake receives. The day I was there, sixteen Cub Scouts were having their fishing lines threaded by their grandfathers. Somebody asked who was going to catch the first fish. All sixteen shouted, "I am!"

48. Asahel Curtis Nature Trail

Type: Day hike
Difficulty: Easy
Hikable: June–October
Loop: 1 one mile
High point: 2,000 feet
Elevation gain: 100 feet
Maps: Green Trails No. 207 Snoqualmie Pass; U.S.
Forest Service Mount Baker–Snoqualmie
Information: North Bend Ranger District (360)888-1421

The Asahel Curtis Nature Trail is a beauty, circling 500 acres of choice old-growth forest. This forest has been preserved as a remnant sample of what was once found everywhere in the Puget Sound basin. Thank the Snoqualmie Valley Garden Club for proposing this nature trail and ensuring its preservation. Then walk the short loop trail with children and point out enormous old Douglas fir, cedar, and hemlocks. Though this bit of beauty was never clear-cut, it was high-graded, meaning that a few choice trees were cut. Children can find 75-year-old stumps, some with loggers' notches carved in their sides where loggers stood to swing their axes and run their saws.

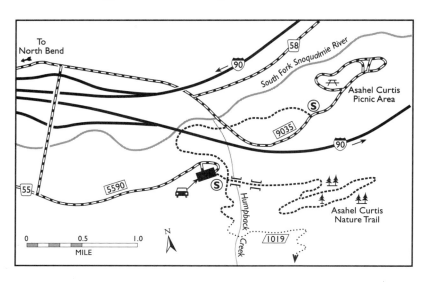

Humpback Creek bridge

From the west, drive I-90 to Exit 47 (Asahel Curtis/Denny Creek exit). At the first stop sign, turn right and, at a crossroads, go left. In 0.5 mile, park in the large Nature Trail–Lake Annette parking lot, elevation 1,900 feet. (There is a second trailhead starting from the Asahel Curtis Picnic Area, adding ¼ mile each way, that may delight a child as it follows the river and ducks under the I-90 freeway. From the west, go right off the freeway, follow signs to the picnic area, and find the trailhead just inside the entrance.)

Find the trailhead in the upper (east) end of the parking lot. In a few feet, beside Humpback Creek, look for a sawdust pile in a hollow cedar, probably made by ants. Cross the creek on a sturdy bridge and, in a few more feet, cross a tributary. Point out some of the enormous,

Asahel Curtis Nature Trail

old Douglas fir trees. Estimate how tall they are to the first limb. Mixed in are cedars, hemlock, and Pacific silver fir. A few 75-year-old stumps dot the forest from back in the 1920s.

Wicked looking devil's club grows 4–5 feet tall. Along the creek edge, look for skunk cabbage, neither a form of cabbage nor particularly bad smelling. A better name would be *swamp lantern* because its bright golden torch seems to light the way. Search for tiny hemlock cones lying on the trail. The larger cones are those of Douglas fir.

Tell the kids the old Indian legend about the mice who, in a time of hunger, looked everywhere for food that humans had hidden. One night they overheard the humans say their stores of grain were kept inside the Douglas fir

Old stump

cones. The mice all ran to the tops of the trees and climbed inside the cones. The cones clamped shut on the mice, leaving only their tails and hind legs exposed. Your children can find tiny legs and tails on the outside of each cone they pick up today. Look for fresh piles of cones left by squirrels who cut out the seeds or nuts.

Note the hemlock that started on a big boulder and now has roots wrapping the rock like latticework. The trail winds through deer ferns and lady ferns and past nurse logs draped in moss and false Solomon's seal, foamflower, youth-on-age, false lily of the valley, trillium, and vanilla leaf. Tell kids that youth-on-age was so named because the new little leaves rise directly out of the large older ones. Try to find the flower of wild ginger. It is well hidden. The miniature Canadian dogwood adds light to the forest floor. At any time of year, creeping twinflower will be visible, but in late summer the telltale tiny, pink double bells will rise above the creeping vine.

In roughly ¼ mile, the trail splits. Take the right trail; the left is the return trail. Pass beside a large boulder with a seat attached. At the upper part of the loop is a dead tree drilled with small woodpecker holes. Near the finish of the loop is a kid's fort, a hollow cedar stump with a slot for a small person to squeeze through and crouch down inside to waylay enemy soldiers, parents, or siblings.

49. Lake Annette

Type: Day hike or backpack
Difficulty: Difficult for children
Hikable: June–October
One way: 4 miles
High point: 3,600 feet
Elevation gain: 1,400 feet
Maps: Green Trails No. 207 Snoqualmie Pass; U.S. Forest Service Mount Baker–Snoqualmie
Information: North Bend Ranger District (360)888-1421

A long, steep woodland trail ascends the valley beneath Silver Peak to a cirque lake fed by waterfalls. Kids enjoy splashing around in the many creeks crossed on the way and playing in the lake-outlet stream.

Drive I-90 to Exit 47 (Asahel Curtis/Denny Creek). At the first stop sign, turn right and, at the second stop sign, turn left. In 0.5 mile, park in the large, paved parking area, elevation 2,400 feet. The trail begins on the east side.

For the first ¾ mile the trail ascends old clear-cuts to the abandoned Milwaukee Railroad grade. Now part of Iron Horse State Park,

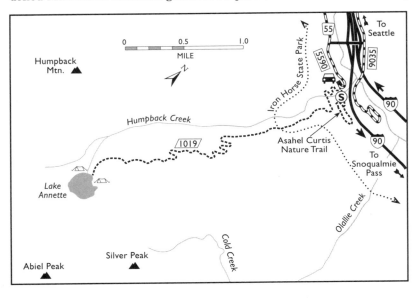

the old railroad grade is now a trail that ultimately may extend to Idaho. A split-log bench is a nice place to rest before starting up a series of steep switchbacks on the western slope of Silver Peak. The trail follows Humpback Creek through stands of large, very old cedar. At one point, the trail is a log 50 feet long and 3 feet wide, with shallow steps cut into it. The last mile is more gradual, crossing rock slides ornamented in spring by clumps of trillium, glacier lily, and Canadian dogwood.

At 4 miles is the lake, elevation 3,600 feet. The north shore is designated "day use only." Campsites are on the shoreline beyond the outlet. There is also camping on the ridge on the south side. Trout fishing is said to be very good.

Humpback Creek

50. Denny Creek Water Slide

Type: Day hike
Difficulty: Easy for children
Hikable: May–November
One way: 1¼ miles
High point: 2,800 feet
Elevation gain: 500 feet
Maps: Green Trails No. 207 Snoqualmie Pass; U.S. Forest Service Mount Baker–Snoqualmie
Information: North Bend Ranger District (360)888-1421
Wilderness permit required

On a hot day, this natural water slide can send children out of their minds with glee. One mother with three kids under seven told me they had played three hours—until the sun went down and they began to feel the cold.

Drive I-90 to Exit 47 (Asahel Curtis/Denny Creek), turn left, and cross the overpass. Turn right on road No. 58, pass Denny Creek Forest Campground, and turn left on road No. 5830 to the signed spur road to the Melakwa Lake trailhead, elevation 2,300 feet.

Trail No. 1014 begins in impressive old forest. At ¼ mile, it crosses a log bridge children will like. They shortly will be astonished to walk under the freeway, to hear cars and trucks rumbling and roaring over their heads, and to peek up through the bridge grates at big black tires rolling by at high speeds. At 1 mile, the trail enters the Alpine Lakes Wilderness, and freeway sounds fade away in the distance. A gradual climb along Denny Creek leads to a section of bedrock, elevation 2,800 feet, where the water spreads out into the water slide.

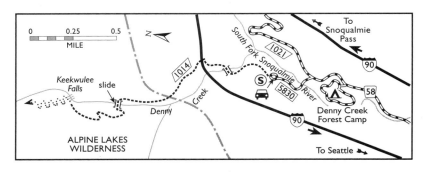

Denny Creek Water Slide

Water volume may be dangerously torrential in the spring, but in later months it dwindles to a gentle and safe flow. At the same time, temperatures rise and kids are attracted like dragonflies. The slide is a wide expanse of bedrock where the creek first narrows to a footstep's width and then widens to slip down the rocky slab. Walk upstream 300 feet to a cascade for children to run under—another exhilarating experience.

51. Franklin Falls

Type: Day hike
Difficulty: Easy for children
Hikable: July–October
One way: ¼ mile, ½ mile, or 1 mile
High point: 2,600 feet
Elevation gain: 100 feet
Maps: Green Trails No. 207 Snoqualmie Pass; U.S. Forest Service Mount Baker–Snoqualmie
Information: North Bend Ranger District (360)888-1421

This is a paradise for kids! Standing beside the 70-foot falls on a warm day, children scream with joy at the cold spray in their faces. The gravel bar and the creek into which the water falls usually are crowded with children wading, splashing, playing on the rocks, and "fishing"—as if the fish would endure such company! Traffic is loud on the Denny Creek section of freeway directly above, but the kids are oblivious to it.

Four trailheads offer routes varying in length from 1 mile to a scant ¼ mile. Parents with toddlers will opt for the shortest way. Those with older children can make the falls a reward after a longer hike.

 Drive I-90 to Exit 47 (Asahel Curtis/Denny Creek). Turn left at the stop sign, crossing the overpasses. At the T, turn right. In ¼ mile, turn left on Denny Creek road No. 58. At 2 miles, pass the Denny Creek Forest Campground and, at 2.25 miles, reach a junction with road No. 5830, signed "Melakwa Lake Trail"; this is the first of the Franklin Falls trailheads. On the right side of the junction, marked

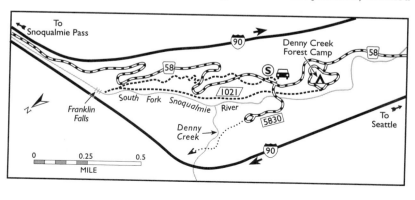

with a wagon wheel, is the historic Snoqualmie Pass Wagon Road, which climbs in 1 mile to Franklin Falls. On the left side, on road No. 5830, is the Franklin Falls trail, also 1 mile in length, starting near the concrete bridge. For a shorter walk, continue up road No. 58 another 0.4 mile to the ½-mile trail to the falls or continue still another 0.5 mile to the ¼-mile trail, also marked with a wagon wheel.

The sometimes muddy ¼-mile trail joins the wagon road and regular trail and then drops to the falls, the final few feet blasted out of solid rock. There is no guardrail, so children will need supervision and young children will need help. The last 200 yards are surfaced with sharp rocks and could be difficult for toddlers to walk through, so parents should plan to carry them here.

Families blink their eyes in disbelief as they see the falls, creek, large gravel bar, and rock walls for the first time. When I was there on a hot summer day, people were picnicking on blankets and folding chairs, watching children happily engrossed in all manner of watery activities.

Franklin Falls

52. Snow Lake

Type: Day hike or backpack
Difficulty: Moderate for children
Hikable: July–October
One way: 4 miles
High point: 4,400 feet
Elevation gain: 1,800 feet in, 400 feet out
Maps: Green Trails No. 207 Snoqualmie Pass; U.S. Forest Service Mount Baker–Snoqualmie
Information: North Bend Ranger District (360)888-1421
Wilderness permit required

Snow Lake is one of the most popular hikes in the Snoqualmie Pass area. The trail, though, is long and steep for children and has endured erosion from the constant stream of hikers. My own kids rebelled at backpacking it when they were eight, nine, and ten, and we bivouacked along the way. But the next day, seeing the lake, they wished they'd kept going and camped there; we returned to do so several times. The rugged and beautiful setting—tall cliffs on one side and vast valley on the other—make it memorable for hikers of all ages.

Drive I-90 to Snoqualmie Pass, turn off on Exit 62, and continue

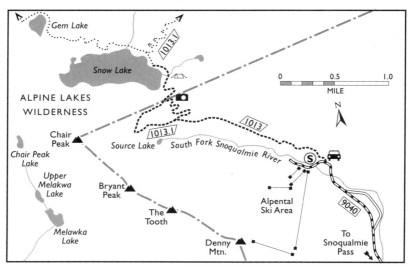

Snow Lake

left 2 miles to the parking lot at the Alpental ski area, elevation 3,100 feet.

Trail No. 1013, starting on the uphill side of the parking lot, is well maintained throughout and has been partly rebuilt recently. At about 2 miles, new short switchbacks have been blasted through rock slides and up through belts of cliffs. The views begin here, down to Source Lake valley and up to the mountains. The track opens out into heather and flowers at Snow Lake saddle, at 4,400 feet. Peaks along the ridge to the west are, from right to left, Chair Peak, the Tooth, Lundin Peak, and Denny Mountain. (Children will want to see in their shapes the reasons for some of their names. Denny, however, has no particular shape; it was named for one of the builders of Seattle.)

From the saddle, the sometimes muddy, slippery trail (watch children carefully) drops 400 feet to the shores of the lake, elevation 4,016 feet, about 4 miles from the parking lot.

The lake is large enough to accommodate a lot of campers, fishermen, photographers, and picnickers and usually does; over 10,000 hikers a year choose it as their destination. To get away from some of the crowds and out of the day-use area to the camping area, try the northeast shoreline beyond the outlet. The views one way are down to the vast gulf of the Middle Fork Snoqualmie and in the other across the lake to snowfields extending to the shore.

145

Snoqualmie Pass Highway: East

Interstate 90

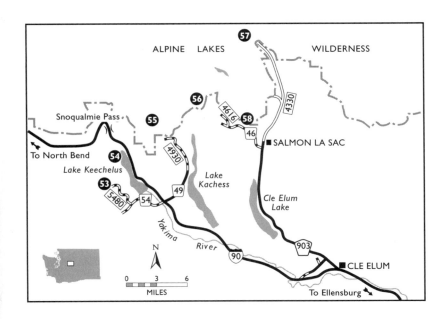

Great horned owl near Snoqualmie Pass

53. Mirror Lake

Type: Day hike or backpack
Difficulty: Easy to moderate for children
Hikable: June–October
One way: 1 mile
High point: 4,200 feet
Elevation gain: 600 feet
Maps: Green Trails No. 207 Snoqualmie Pass; U.S. Forest Service Wenatchee
Information: Cle Elum Ranger District (509)674-4411

This large, clear blue mountain lake lies at the foot of Tinkham Peak. Fishermen, backpacking families, and climbers all find something to enjoy. I saw one fisherman with a nineteen-inch rainbow trout on his line and a smile on his face. This is a "hikers only" trail, rough in places, muddy in others, with several small streams to cross. Fortunately, the trail is short, so little legs should be able to manage.

 Drive I-90 east of Snoqualmie Pass to Stampede Pass Exit 62. Turn south on road No. 54, pass Crystal Springs Campground, cross the Yakima River bridge, and at 1.2 miles go right on road No. 5480. Stay on this road and, at 5.2 miles, reach a five-way junction. Take the second road to the right, pass Lost Lake, and continue another 2.2 miles to the trailhead, elevation 3,600 feet.

Trail No. 1302 begins in a clear-cut but in 200 yards enters old-growth forest and at ½ mile reaches shallow Cottonwood Lake,

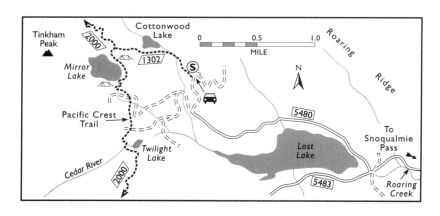

Mirror Lake

beneath the open slopes of Roaring Ridge. Camping and wading are possible here.

Continue another ½ mile, passing large boulders, to Mirror Lake, elevation 4,200 feet. Clear and deep, with eleven campsites on both its north and south ends (and a few in the middle), Mirror Lake reflects whatever a hiker wants to see. Gaze upward 1,000 feet to the crags of Tinkham Peak or visit the waterfall below the lake's outfall stream.

54. The Spook of the Iron Horse Trail

Type:	Day hike
Difficulty:	Easy for children
Hikable:	June–October
One way:	to tunnel, ¾ mile
One way:	to Lake Keechelus, ¾ mile
High point:	2,550 feet
Elevation gain:	None
Map:	U.S. Forest Service Mount Baker–Snoqualmie Forest

Walk a level, abandoned railroad grade to view a spooky tunnel. Children can walk into the dark, dripping cavity as far as they wish and then turn and retrace their steps along the Lake Keechelus trail. The trail is wide and popular with hikers and bicycle riders. By staying out of the way of the bicyclists, families with small children can enjoy the tunnel section of what is called the Iron Horse Trail, after the Milwaukee–St. Paul Railroad, which ran here until the mid-1970s. Be sure to bring jackets, hats, and flashlights for everyone for the tunnel. The trip is best done on a cloudy day since there is no shade along the way.

    Drive I-90 to Snoqualmie Pass and continue on to the Hyak Exit 54. Look for brown signs directing you to the Lake Keechelus trailhead and the Iron Horse Trail, elevation 2,600 feet.

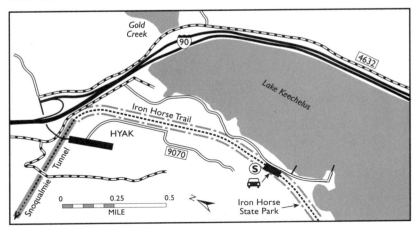

Begin by walking west on crushed rock for ¾ mile. Just before the tunnel entrance, find an old boxcar on its side with metal relics of old railroad days. The top of the tunnel reads, "Snoqualmie Tunnel—1912–1914," indicating the years it took to build it. The tunnel is 2½ miles long, which is too long a distance for most families to hike in total darkness, but some children will enjoy a brief sojourn into the spooky interior to listen to the hollow-sounding echoes down its length. Showers of cold water cascade from the roof, splashing hikers and bicyclists alike. The deeper you go, the more the temperature drops and the darker it gets. Even good flashlights seem to dim as daylight recedes. **CAUTION** Keep the kids well lighted and out of the way of reckless bicyclists.

When the kids have had enough, turn around and find out how wonderful daylight is. For more adventure, walk east past the trailhead parking lot toward Lake Keechelus. Keechelus was logged when it became a reservoir, leaving stumps along its fluctuating shoreline. The shoreline is reached in ¾ mile.

Inside the Snoqualmie Tunnel

55. Rachel Lake

Type: Day hike or backpack
Difficulty: Difficult for children
Hikable: July–October
One way: 4 miles
High point: 4,700 feet
Elevation gain: 1,900 feet
Maps: Green Trails No. 207 Snoqualmie Pass; U.S. Forest Service Wenatchee
Information: Cle Elum Ranger District (509)674-4411
Wilderness permit required

 The outstanding beauty of this exquisite alpine lake carved from the side of Rampart Ridge draws hundreds of hikers, many with small children, every summer weekend. Yet this is one of the toughest-to-walk trails in the Cascades and definitely not for inexperienced hikers. The way is clearly marked but be prepared for rocks, roots, mud, and crawl-over logs. Adults and older kids frequently do Rachel Lake as a day hike, but it's better as a 3-day trip. Carry a stove because campfires are prohibited at all lakes.

 Drive I-90 east of Snoqualmie Pass and take the Lake Kachess Exit 62. Follow signs north 5 miles to Lake Kachess Campground, turn left on Box Canyon road No. 4930, and go 4 miles to a junction. Turn left, drive 0.2 mile, and park in the lot at the trailhead, elevation 2,800 feet.

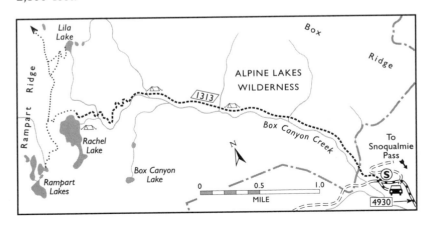

Rachel Lake

Rachel Lake trail No. 1313 leaves the upper side of the parking lot in a forest filled with huckleberries. The tread is rough and narrow, contouring a sidehill toward Box Canyon Creek. At ½ mile, the trail improves somewhat, entering the Alpine Lakes Wilderness. You'll find campsites at 1 mile. Follow the trail along the creek the next 2 miles, always within sight and sound of it. At 2½ miles, the trail crosses several streams and switchbacks uphill beside a waterfall, a good place to rest and cool hands and faces in anticipation of the next 1½ miles—"the cruel mile"—that will climb 1,300 feet. At about 3 miles, the trail passes under a waterfall—another good resting point, with a free shower thrown in. (Some children go wild, soaking heads, feet, or even entire bodies in the falls.) From here, the trail is at its worst, climbing over rocks, boulders, and roots and up streambeds until, at 4 miles, the grade abruptly levels out at deep blue Rachel Lake, elevation 4,700 feet. Numerous campsites are scattered on both sides of the outlet stream.

If your children (and you) survive the trail to Rachel Lake, the middle day of a 3-day trip can be the best. From the lake outlet, climb the boot-beaten trail to the right, ascending 600 feet up the very steep mountainside to the broad saddle between Rampart Ridge and Alta Mountain. Take the trail left for an up-and-down ½ mile to Rampart Lakes, a magnificent chain set in glacier-scoured bedrock bowls. Children can wade, swim, and throw rocks; parents can sketch or photograph these picture-perfect settings.

56. Pete Lake

Type: Backpack
Difficulty: Moderate for children
Hikable: July–October
High point: 2,980 feet
Elevation gain: 200 feet
Maps: Green Trails No. 208 Lake Kachess; U.S. Forest Service Wenatchee
Information: Cle Elum Ranger District (509)674-4411
Wilderness permit required

Large, woodland Pete Lake makes a popular family campsite at the end of a gentle trail through old-growth forest. Children will joyfully throw sticks and stones in three or four creeks along the way. At the lake, they can also wade and swim, because the water, while not warm, is also not ice cold. Because there is no special turnaround point, this hike is best for an overnight trip.

Drive I-90 east of Snoqualmie Pass and turn off on Exit 80, signed "Salmon la Sac–Roslyn." Follow the county road, through Roslyn and Ronald and along Cle Elum Lake for 16 miles. Turn left on Cooper Lake road No. 46, go 4.7 miles, and turn right on road No. 4616. Cross Cooper River on a cement bridge, pass a campground and boat launch, and at 1.8 miles from road No. 46 hit the trailhead, elevation 2,800 feet.

Cooper River trail No. 1323 joins a lakeshore path and winds through virgin timber and undergrowth. At about 4 miles is a giant

Raccoon

Pete Lake

rock slide and the last little climb before reaching the lake, elevation 2,980 feet.

To the west of the lake are exciting views of Overcoat and Bears Breast mountains. I have pictures of my three children beneath the peaks sitting on a log eating their breakfast porridge like the three bears.

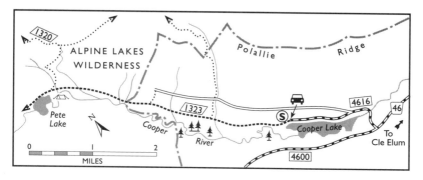

57. Hyas Lakes

Type: Day hike or backpack
Difficulty: Easy for children
Hikable: June–November
One way: to Hyas Lake, 1½ miles
One way: to Little Hyas Lake, 2½ miles
High point: 3,450 feet
Elevation gain: 50 feet
Maps: Green Trails No. 176 Stevens Pass; U.S. Forest Service Wenatchee
Information: Cle Elum Ranger District (509)674-4411
Wilderness permit required

Two large forested lakes—very popular and with campsites almost beyond counting—wait at the end of a gradual trail through fine old timber. From camps near the shores of either Hyas or Little Hyas lakes or from the swampy reed-filled area between the two, searches can be made for frogs, newts, and salamanders. As the numbers of these creatures are dwindling at alarming rates, discourage children from catching and injuring them or disturbing their eggs. Cathedral Rock rises a striking 6,000 feet above the west shores.

Drive I-90 east of Snoqualmie Pass and turn at Exit 80, signed "Salmon la Sac–Roslyn." Go 3 miles and turn left on county road No. 903. Wind through the old mining town of Roslyn and pass Lake Cle Elum, a small natural lake made into a huge reservoir whose level fluctuates. At 17 miles from Roslyn, just beyond the Salmon la Sac Guard Station, go right on unpaved road No. 4330. Drive 15 more miles to its end and Hyas Lakes trail No. 1376, elevation 3,400 feet.

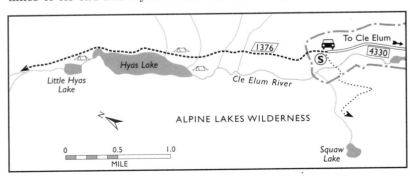

The trail is nearly flat and so wide that hikers can walk abreast. Three or four creeks can be difficult to cross in the high waters of early summer, but later they make good spots to rest or play. An easy 1½-mile trek leads to the larger of the two Hyas lakes. Another easy mile more reaches Little Hyas Lake, elevation 3,450 feet.

Campsites are scattered along both lakes. The first lakeshore camp has the best swimming beach, but you must arrive very early (preferably by Friday evening) to have a chance to get it. Note that the sandy beach ends in an abrupt drop-off, so keep a careful eye on nonswimmers. Some camps at Little Hyas Lake are large enough for several congenial families to camp together. Downed logs and the exposed roots of enormous old trees provide play places for children and their real or imaginary friends.

Hyas Lake

58. Cooper Lake and River Walk

Type: Day hike
Difficulty: Moderate
Hikable: June–October
One way: 4 miles
High point: 2,800 feet
Elevation gain: 400 feet
Map: Green Trails No. 208 Kachess Lake
Information: Cle Elum Ranger District (509)674-4411

This trail parallels a road, mostly out of sight. Ride if you will, but you and the children will miss out on some good things. A sylvan walk along the Cooper River leads families through old-growth forest land, some of which is owned by a timber company but proposed for a land exchange. Clear-cuts are visible across the river on steep hillsides. The trail leads to lovely Cooper Lake lying alongside the Alpine Lakes Wilderness. Children were wading and floating on inner tubes when we were there.

In 1864, the government granted as a reward to the builders of railroads free land for 40 miles on either side of the railroad in a checkerboard pattern. Plum Creek Timber is the inheritor of this giveaway today, but the U.S. Forest Service is trying to arrange for an even exchange of land so the entire valley will belong in the Wenatchee National Forest. The trail drops to a road alongside Cooper Lake, where children can wade and swim.

 Drive I-90 east of Snoqualmie Pass to Exit 80, signed "Salmon la Sac–Roslyn." Go 3 miles and turn left on county road No. 903. Sixteen miles beyond Roslyn, cross a bridge and reach the Salmon la Sac Campground. Just beyond the bridge, turn right to find the

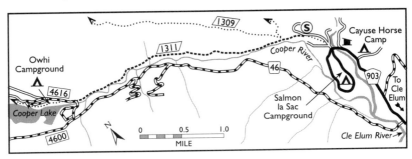

Cooper River

trailhead, elevation 2,800 feet. If you wish to leave a car at the lake for return transportation, drive a mile south of the Salmon la Sac Campground, turn right on Cooper River road No. 46 for 4.7 miles to Cooper Lake Junction, and then go left on road No. 4616 until you reach the lake. Cross the Cooper River on a bridge and find the end of the trail.

Begin in a Plum Creek Timber checkerboard section of forest. To avoid building roads, the timber company lifted these logs out by helicopters. On a hot July day, teenagers were swinging on a rope over a deep pool and then dropping into the cold water. At 1½ miles, the trail drops down to the river again and a campsite for one or two parties. Forest flowers include lupine, pipsissewa, wild roses, vanilla leaf (which when dried smells sweet), tiger lily, and twining twinflowers. The old-growth forest of fir, hemlock, and silver fir, offers cool shade on a hot day, and the sound of rapids and rushing water is never distant. Reach the lake at 4 miles, cross a graveled access road, and find a large drive-in campground with swimming and boating nearby.

On Burroughs Mountain

Chinook Pass Highway: West

State Route 410

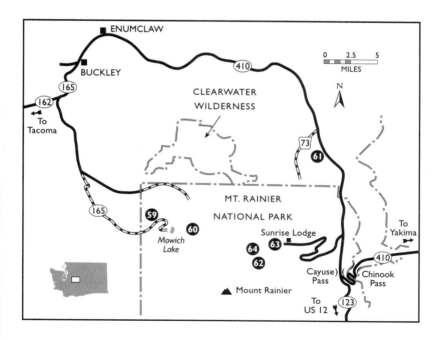

59. Eunice Lake

Type: Day hike
Difficulty: Easy for children
Hikable: Mid-July–October
One way: 1¾ miles
High point: 5,354 feet
Elevation gain: 500 feet in, 200 feet out
Maps: Green Trails No. 269 Mount Rainier West; Mount Rainier National Park Backcountry Trip Planner
Information: Mount Rainier National Park (360)569-2211, ext. 3317

One of the loveliest alpine lakes in Mount Rainier National Park is reached by a short hike from Mowich Lake. Above Eunice, a steep, short trail climbs to the Tolmie Peak lookout. Children are perfectly enchanted by Eunice Lake as well. One hot day I heard a mother ask who wanted to climb to the summit; four children playing on the shore replied in unison, "Not me!"

Follow Highways 162 and 165 through Wilkeson and Carbonado, past the high, narrow bridge over the Carbon River, to the fork beyond. Keep right at the fork and follow the road to its end at Mowich Lake, elevation 4,929 feet. Park along the road where it crosses the pass from which Mowich Lake is first visible. The trail to Eunice Lake heads north from the road. If there is no parking at the pass, continue downhill to the road-end parking lot at the lake and pick up the trail there.

Actually, two trails depart from the parking lot. The trail to Spray Park (Hike 60) heads downhill from the walk-in campsite on the south side of Mowich Lake near the outlet stream. The trail to Eunice Lake— here a short segment of the Wonderland Trail—begins on the opposite side of the parking lot. It rounds the lakeshore through old-growth noble and silver firs and Alaska cedars and then parallels the nearby road to the pass just mentioned. At 1½ miles is a junction. The Wonderland Trail goes right over Ipsut Pass. Your way goes left on the Eunice Lake trail but take the time to walk the Wonderland Trail a few feet to look out over the Carbon River valley.

The trail to Eunice Lake drops 100 feet to skirt a cliff and then climbs ½ mile to berry-filled meadows and the lake, 5,354 feet. Mount Rainier is suddenly and vastly apparent.

Eunice Lake and Mount Rainier

If children can bear to leave the water play, the 1-mile hike to Tolmie Peak lookout (with a 600-foot elevation gain) gives grandly spectacular views. Look north for Mount Baker and east for Glacier Peak and almost reach out to touch Rainier. Plan the hike for a warm day in late summer when berries are ripe; cool off by wading or dunking in the lake.

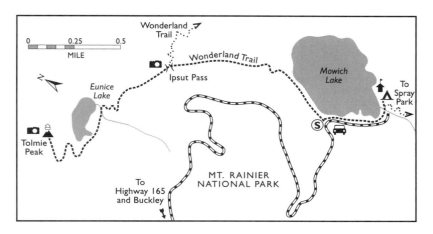

60. Spray Park

Type: Day hike or backpack
Difficulty: Moderate for children
Hikable: Mid-July–October
One way: 2¾ miles
High point: 5,700 feet
Elevation gain: 1,100 feet in, 300 feet out
Maps: Green Trails No. 269 Mount Rainier West;
Mount Rainier National Park Backcountry
Trip Planner
Information: Mount Rainier National Park (360)569-2211,
ext. 3317
Backcountry permit required for camping

Some of the most exquisite flower meadows on the north side of Mount Rainier National Park can be attained for a small expenditure of energy. Views of "The Mountain" above fields of avalanche lilies here are unforgettable. Though there is no camping in Spray Park, families can camp in the woods at Eagle's Roost and then do the higher day trips above.

From Buckley drive to the parking lot at Mowich Lake (see Hike 59).

Start from the walk-in campsite south of the lake. The beginning is on the Wonderland Trail, which drops ½ mile to a junction. Go left

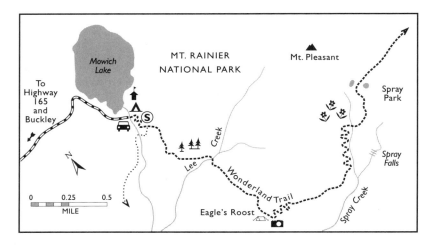

on the Spray Park trail, wide and gently graded, through a forest of immense old-growth noble and silver fir. At 1½ miles, stop to peer over Eagle Cliff. Children will be astonished to find themselves on top of a precipice with views across a deep valley to the snouts of the Mowich and Russell glaciers.

Just beyond is the campsite at Eagle's Roost. At 2 miles, a side trail goes off ¼ mile to Spray Falls—well worth the trip to eat lunch with more views, in a cooling mist from the falls.

Back on the trail, the last ¾ mile switchbacks steeply upward 600 feet to the meadows of Spray Park, elevation 5,700 feet.

Here one can see avalanche lilies in June; lupine, anemones, and paintbrush in mid-July; and asters and gentian in August. Blueberries continue into September. Some of the flower meadows are fringed with small subalpine firs that are encroaching, but nowadays the timberline is here, at the meadow edge, and as hikers continue upward, the views open wider and wider, until trees disappear altogether.

Avalanche lilies and Mount Rainier at Spray Park

61. Skookum Flats

Type: Day hike
Difficulty: Easy
Hikable: Most of the year
One way: to Skookum Creek Falls, 2 miles
One way: to suspension bridge, 4¼miles
High point: 2,460 feet
Elevation gain: 300 feet
Maps: Green Trails No. 238 Greenwater
Information: White River Ranger District (360)825-6585

A beautiful old-growth woodland walk leads along the White River to a waterfall or, if two cars are available, a bouncy suspension bridge back to the highway. There are a number of river-level campsites and lunch stops where children can safely play in streams and pools.

Volunteers from the Washington Trails Association spent days restoring this trail after the disastrous floods of 1995. Families should know that this trail is popular with mountain bicyclists. The majority are friendly and courteous, but caution is advised.

Drive Highway 410 east of Enumclaw for 34 miles and go right on road No. 73 (poorly marked in 1996). Cross the White River and immediately find the parking area on the right and the Skookum Flats trail No. 1194 on the left, elevation 2,160 feet. Note the piles of trees on wide gravel bars that show the power of the 1995–96 winter floods.

For the pickup point 4 miles upstream, follow Highway 410 past the Dalles Campground at 1 mile and a Boy Scout Camp at 3½ miles and find the pickup point at 3.8 miles. A small parking spot is on the left side, and an unmarked trailhead is on the right.

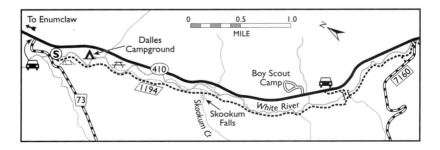

The trail immediately enters a forest of enormous firs and cedars that will cause you to strain your neck looking up. At your feet are prince's pine, Indian pipes, vanilla leaf, foamflower, twisted stalk, and devil's club. The first campsite is close to the road, but floods have made the river inaccessible. Until the next flood, find nice spots at 1 and 1½ miles. At 2 miles, reach Skookum Creek; upstream out of sight is Skookum Creek Falls. During the summer months, White River is best called "Mud River." Explain to your children that the mud is Mount Rainier flowing by. Explain how the glaciers on the mountain scour the soft volcanic rock, and as the glaciers melt, they load the river with their silt, giving it the milky appearance.

Columbia ground squirrel

62. Glacier Basin

Type: Day hike or backpack
Difficulty: Difficult for children
Hikable: Mid-July–October
One way: 3½ miles
High point: 6,000 feet
Elevation gain: 1,700 feet
Maps: Green Trails No. 270 Mount Rainier East; Mount Rainier National Park Backcountry Trip Planner
Information: Mount Rainier National Park (360)569-2211, ext. 3317
Backcountry permit required for camping

The meadow at Glacier Basin is a marmot metropolis. Elk graze in the lush grass; goats frequently amble on the ridge above, sometimes by the dozens. But perhaps the most exciting wildlife is the ubiquitous mountain climber, sure to be seen on summer weekends, usually in enormous numbers, on the way to or from the summit of Mount Rainier. There are also the ghosts of the prospectors who began digging here at the turn of the century and now have vanished completely

   Drive Highway 410 east from Enumclaw toward Chinook Pass. Enter Mount Rainier National Park, continue to the White River Entrance Station, and then go 5 miles more, cross the White River, and turn left on the White River Campground road. Go to the road's end, elevation 4,300 feet.

   The trail begins at the upper end of the last campground loop on a miners' road, used until the 1950s, beside the glacier-silted Inter Fork White River. Much of the way, the old roadbed is wide enough for two to walk abreast. Children may see evidence of porcupine scratches low down on older tree trunks. The trail climbs alongside the Emmons Glacier moraine. At 1 mile, a side trail to the left crosses Inter Fork and climbs to a viewpoint of the snout of the Emmons Glacier and out over the immense expanse of ice, strewn with enormous rocks from the avalanche that swept across the glacier from Little Tahoma in 1964.

After the intersection with the side trail, the path narrows to true trail, climbing through forest and rejoining the old road at about 2¼ miles. At 2½ miles is a switchback; look for some wheels and piles of rotten boards, the remains of the Starbo Mine's power generator.

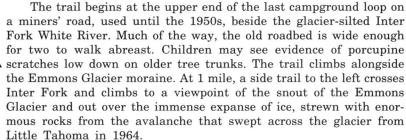

Marmot beside Glacier Basin Trail

The steep final mile levels out at last in Glacier Basin at 3½ miles, elevation 6,000 feet. Campsites are everywhere, if you choose to stay.

Watch for summit parties loaded with high-tech equipment for climbing glaciers. Continue into the meadowy basin and watch for hoary marmots. Children can whistle to them and think they are being answered by a network of marmot cousins; in fact, each "extended family" has a lookout marmot posted, usually on a big rock. They pick up and pass on other whistles whenever one spots an intruder who resembles a bear or coyote.

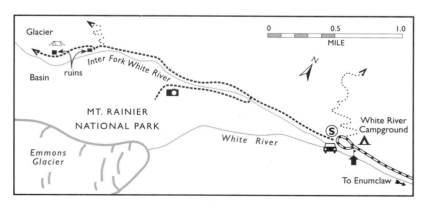

63. Shadow Lake Trail

Type: Day hike
Difficulty: Easy for children
Hikable: Mid-July–October
One way: 1½ miles
High point: 6,100 feet
Elevation gain: 200 feet in, 200 feet out
Maps: Green Trails No. 270 Mount Rainier East; Mount Rainier National Park East Backcountry Trip Planner
Information: Mount Rainier National Park (360)569-2211, ext. 3317

This hike offers flowers, meadows, ground squirrels, marmots, Christmas trees in a parkland setting, plus a shallow lake for wading—all this with your choice between a gated road and a delightful trail. A spectacular view of the Emmons Glacier can be thrown in.

Drive Highway 410 east from Enumclaw to the White River Entrance Station of Mount Rainier National Park. From the station, drive to the end of the road at the Sunrise Visitor Center parking lot, elevation 6,400 feet.

Find the gated service road at the southwest corner of the parking lot. Either walk the sometimes too-hot road or the usually cool, shadowed trail. Both start at the same place, both distances are the same, both lose 200 feet, and both end up in a walk-in campground. The trail is by far the more pleasant. It has some ups and downs but also the best flowers, and the tread is smooth. Views of Rainier are good. At 1½ miles, you reach Shadow Lake, amid meadows and neatly

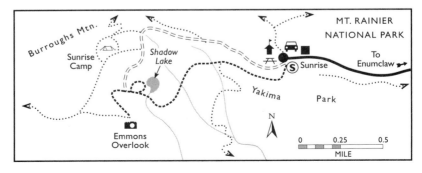

Shadow Lake Trail

trimmed subalpine trees. Explain to the kids how they are shaped by nature to shed the heavy winter snow.

For most people, the lake is far enough. Children love wading and watching for the polliwogs and frogs. Should your family be ready to see still more, ½ mile farther and 300 feet higher is one of the most spectacular vistas of the Emmons Glacier. Follow the trail ⅛ mile to the walk-in campground and follow the Burroughs Mountain trail to the first viewpoint (Hike 64).

64. Burroughs Mountain

Type: Day hike
Difficulty: Moderate for children
Hikable: Mid-July–September
One way: to First Burroughs, 1¼ miles
One way: to Second Burroughs, 1¾ miles
High point: 7,400 feet
Elevation gain: 900 feet
Maps: Green Trails No. 270 Mount Rainier East; Mount Rainier National Park Backcountry Trip Planner
Information: Mount Rainier National Park (360)569-2211, ext. 3317

Burroughs Mountain is so close to Mount Rainier's gigantic north side glaciers it seems to run right into them—in fact, it looks down on their lower paths to crevasses and around the corner to the base of Willis Wall. Some seasons, snow patches linger late on the trail and are very dangerous, so call ahead to ask the ranger if the snow is gone.

 Sometimes they are perilous even when the trail is legally "open." The trail is wide and, aside from the patches, smooth and well maintained. There may be an icy wind, so be sure to carry extra clothing for the summit.

 Drive to Sunrise Visitor Center (see Hike 63), elevation 6,400 feet. Two trails from the parking lot go to First Burroughs Mountain. Each has a steep, dangerous snow patch that seldom melts before August and some years doesn't melt at all. When the snow is gone, the upper trail past Frozen Lake is the easier, but the snow often stays longer

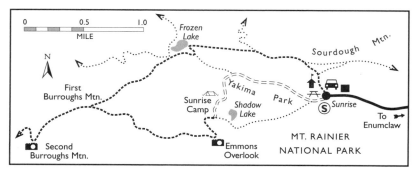

Mount Rainier from Burroughs Mountain. Little Tahoma and Emmons Glacier on left, Steamboat Prow center right, and Winthrop Glacier on right.

on this north-facing slope. The lower route past Sunrise Camp loses 200 feet before climbing, but its snow faces south and thus melts earlier.

Sunrise Camp Route: From the southwest corner of the parking lot, take the service road or the trail to Sunrise Camp. Both ways are about 1½ miles and lose some 200 feet. At the campsites, find the trail, which climbs steeply upwards to Burroughs Mountain. In ¼ mile is a magnificent overlook of the White River and Emmons Glacier. Views get even better higher on the trail, which climbs 900 feet to First Burroughs and then joins the Frozen Lake trail.

Frozen Lake Route: From the picnic area behind the rest rooms at Sunrise, the trail climbs steeply up Sourdough Ridge, gaining 400 feet.

Clark's nutcracker

Stay left at the trail junction to reach Frozen Lake (actually a reservoir) and a junction of five trails. Take the trail on the left and follow it up along the rocky slopes of First Burroughs Mountain. Round a slope of andesite lava slabs and pass (or turn back at) the late snowfield and in ¾ mile attain the plateau summit of First Burroughs Mountain, at 7,300 feet, and the junction with the Sunrise Camp trail.

First Burroughs, a plateau as flat as a surveyor's table, overlooks the Emmons, Carbon, and Winthrop glaciers. The reason it has so little plant life is that the moisture from rain and snowmelt drain underground, creating an arid condition here. The result is true tundra—a special alpine plant community like that in northern Alaska. The scattered plants have a hard time surviving and must not be stepped on. Children (and parents) should stay on the marked paths to give the plants a fighting chance.

The trail dips a little and then climbs again and ½ mile from the First Burroughs junction reaches the summit of Second Burroughs Mountain, elevation 7,400 feet. Here the views expand outward to Grand Park, Moraine Park, Frozen Lake, and Glacier Basin and upward to Interglacier, Steamboat Prow, and the chains of summit climbers moving slowly up or down. Tell the children a glacier is a great river of ice filled with crevasses caused both by the flow of ice moving more swiftly in the center than on the sides and by the resistance of boulders underneath.

Chinook Pass Highway: East

State Route 410

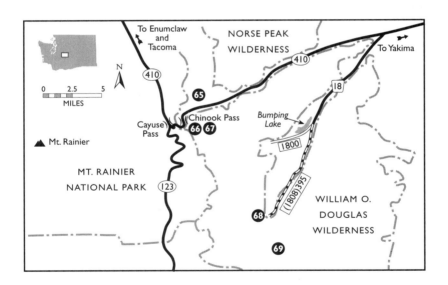

65. Sheep Lake

Type: Day hike or backpack
Difficulty: Easy for children
Hikable: Mid-July–October
One way: 2 miles
High point: 5,700 feet
Elevation gain: 300 feet in, 100 feet out
Maps: Green Trails No. 270 Mount Rainier East;
U.S. Forest Service Wenatchee
Information: Naches Ranger District (509)653-2205

A sidehill trail offers an easy stroll through meadowland to a delightful lake surrounded on three sides by cliffs. (I talked to a mother who was proud that her 3-year-old had walked three-quarters of the way and to a 5-year-old who had walked all the way, carrying his own small pack.) Kids love looking for polliwogs along the shallow shoreline.

Drive Highway 410 east from Enumclaw to the parking area

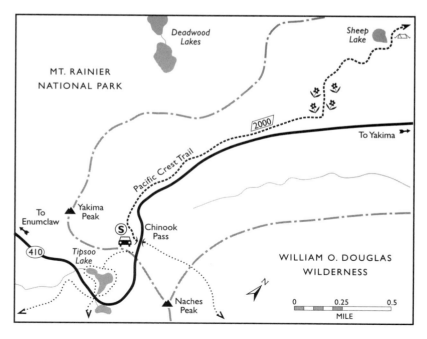

0.25 mile east of Chinook Pass summit, just outside the Mount Rainier National Park entrance, elevation 5,432 feet. Find the Pacific Crest trailhead to the north of the old wooden overpass.

The trail heads north, paralleling the highway and dropping slightly. The trail was blasted into the steep and rocky hillside, so sometimes it's a little rough. This is part of the Pacific Crest Trail, which is open to horses; while there are few horses, meeting one on a narrow trail on the steep hillside is very uncomfortable. There is no way the horse can turn around or back up, so the hiker must do so. At 1¼ miles, the trail diverges from the highway, the tread becomes smooth, and a gentle ascent through a little meadow with trees leads to Sheep Lake, elevation 5,700 feet.

Campsites are scattered around the shore and above the outlet. For better views, although not of Mount Rainier, hike another mile to Sourdough Gap.

Sheep Lake

66. Naches Peak Loop

Type: Day hike
Difficulty: Moderate for children
Hikable: Mid-July–October
Loop: 5 miles
High point: 5,800 feet
Elevation gain: 600 feet
Maps: Green Trails No. 270 Mount Rainier East and No. 271 Bumping Lake; Mount Rainier National Park Backcountry Trip Planner
Information: Mount Rainier National Park (360)569-2211, ext. 3317
Wilderness permit required

A dream hike for families. Children love picking berries along the easy trail and playing in the warm, shallow pond at its highest point. Parents will be inspired by the magnificence of the views. Small ponds and an early-season waterfall invite children to a ducking of some kind or, on a hot day, a full shower. The trail is gently graded and, except for the early-season snow patches, is a cinch for toddlers. Older kids may engage in snowball warfare.

Drive Highway 410 east from Enumclaw through Mount Rainier

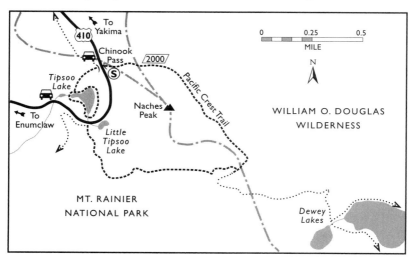

National Park to 0.25 mile east of the Chinook Pass summit. A large parking lot provides safer parking than the roadside, but you will need to walk back to the wooden overpass at 5,432 feet.

Walk across the overpass, then contour the east side of Naches Peak and enter the William O. Douglas Wilderness. Pass a small pond and climb over a 5,800-foot spur ridge.

The way then drops a bit, enters Mount Rainier National Park, and at 1½ miles comes to a junction. The left fork drops to the Dewey Lakes (Hike 67). Go right, into a grand sprawl of alpine meadows. The stupefying views of Mount Rainier are framed by flowers, subalpine trees, and clumps of beargrass. Look for pink Indian paintbrush, gray-bearded anemones (Old Man of the Mountain) gone to seed, lavender phlox, white valerian, and golden arnica. At 2 miles is a small, warm lake that cries out to be circled, tested, and waded in. From here the continuation of the loop is all downhill to Tipsoo Lakes. The driver (only) must then walk up the highway ¼ mile, gaining 150 feet, to the parked car.

Naches Peak Trail and Mount Rainier

67. Dewey Lakes

Type:	Day hike or backpack
Difficulty:	Moderate for children
Hikable:	July–October
One way:	2¾ miles
High point:	5,800 feet
Elevation gain:	300 feet in, 700 feet out
Maps:	Green Trails No. 270 Mount Rainier East and No. 271 Bumping Lake; U.S. Forest Service Wenatchee
Information:	Naches Ranger District (509)653-2205
	Wilderness permit required

This hike offers a little bit of everything kids love. To begin, the trail crosses the highway on an old wooden overpass. What child can resist the appeal of a high traverse over the highway? There are also summer snowbanks for sliding and snowballing, a waterfall, and two wading and swimming lakes to camp by.

From Enumclaw or Yakima, drive Highway 410 to Chinook Pass to a parking lot just outside the entrance to Mount Rainier National Park, elevation 5,432 feet.

Walk across the overpass bridge and head south on the Pacific

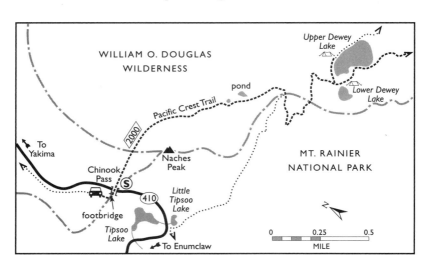

Small tarn on Pacific Crest Trail on way to Dewey Lakes

Crest Trail, contouring the slope of Naches Peak. You enter the William
O. Douglas Wilderness and pass an unnamed pond—be sure to check
it for polliwogs. There are many early-summer snow patches, so prepare
for snowball fights. (The snow generally lasts until the start of August.)
At about 1 mile, watch for a waterfall on the right, where on a warm
day in early summer a cooling shower may be taken.

The trail is mostly smooth, featuring an easy 10 percent grade to
a 5,800-foot high point. At 1½ miles, the Naches Peak loop trail (Hike
66) goes right. You also have your first good look at Mount Rainier.
Keep left on the Pacific Crest Trail, signed "Dewey Lakes." Descend
700 feet on long switchbacks with occasional views of Rainier. The
destination is a meadow between Upper and Lower Dewey lakes,
elevation 5,100 feet.

If you want to linger overnight, excellent campsites lie around
both lakeshores. The flower fields are famous when in full bloom,
which in an average year is mid-July to early August.

68. Twin Sisters Lakes

Type: Day hike or backpack
Difficulty: Easy for children
Hikable: Mid-July–October
One way: to Little Twin, 1¾ miles
One way: to Big Twin, 2¼ miles
High point: 5,200 feet
Elevation gain: 900 feet
Maps: Green Trails No. 271 Bumping Lake and No. 303 White Pass; U.S. Forest Service Wenatchee
Information: Naches Ranger District (509)653-2205
Wilderness permit required

These two large jewel-like lakes lie close together on a well-graded trail, close enough to the road for a day trip, but delightful enough to deserve an overnight at one of the many excellent campsites. They are among the largest mountain lakes in the state and are protected as part of the William O. Douglas Wilderness. In season, the alpine flowers are wonderful; blueberries, huckleberries, and ground whortleberries ripen in late summer.

 Take Highway 410 west from Yakima or 19 miles east from Chinook Pass and turn south on the Bumping River road. Go 11 miles to Bumping Lake and then follow road No. 1800 (county road 2008) to the junction with road No. 1808(395). Keep straight ahead, following No. 1808(395) past the first Twin Sisters Lakes trailhead, and at 7 miles reach the second Twin Sisters Lakes trailhead at Deep Creek Campground, elevation 4,300 feet.

The trail is kept in good condition. The first half has a gentle grade; the last half steepens at 1¾ miles to Little Twin Sister Lake, with its sandy beaches and lovely inlets and coves. The best campsites are near the outlet, elevation 5,200 feet.

The trail proceeds ½ mile, losing 50 feet, to Big Twin Sister Lake, elevation 5,152 feet. Twice the size of the little sister, it too has great campsites at the outlet. Between the two lakes are numerous frog ponds and, of course, flowers by the thousands. Horses' hooves have trampled parts of the trail into mire.

For a panoramic view of the William O. Douglas Wilderness, overnighters can climb to the old lookout site atop Tumac Mountain, an extinct (we hope) volcano. Cross the outlet of Little Twin Sister

Little Twin Sister Lake

Lake and follow trail No. 44. In ⅓ mile keep right at a junction and continue 2 miles on the Tumac Mountain trail. The trail starts on a gentle grade and then steepens as it spirals up to the 6,340-foot summit, 1,200 feet above the lake.

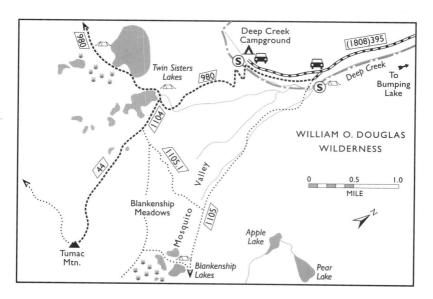

69. William O. Douglas Wilderness Vacation

Type: Backpack
Difficulty: Moderate for children
Hikable: July–October
Loop: 30 miles
High point: 5,400 feet
Elevation gain: 2,500 feet
Maps: Green Trails No. 303 White Pass and No. 271 Bumping Lake; U.S. Forest Service Wenatchee
Information: Naches Ranger District (509)653-2205
Wilderness permit required

It's such beautiful country and there are so many delightful spots, I recommend it for a week-long vacation. Because it is horse country, some sections of the trail are a quagmire, especially early in the season when the ground is soft. Justice William O. Douglas spent much of

Little Twin Sister Lake

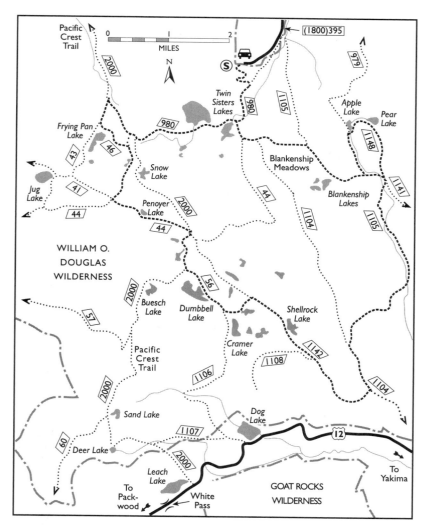

his leisure time—from boyhood until he was past 70 years of age—
exploring this area, preserved now for us and our children. You may
want to set up a base camp at Twin Sisters Lakes and then visit other
nearby lakes each day. Or, in early season, when water is plentiful,
this trip can be done as a grand loop. However, when water is plentiful, so are mosquitoes, thousands and thousands of them, each with
an enormous appetite. For that reason, even though the peak of the
flower season may be past, mid-August to September is the most
pleasant time to backpack in this area.

Big Twin Sister Lake

For the loop, drive to the second Twin Sisters Lakes trailhead (see Hike 68). Hike the 1½ miles to Little Twin Sister Lake (Hike 68), your first camp. From there, take trail No. 980 downhill 2 miles to the Pacific Crest Trail, turn north, and go 1 mile. Turn left on trail No. 43 and go ½ mile to a camp at Frying Pan Lake. For the third stage, take trail No. 46, and turn on No. 44. Pass Penoyer Lake and continue to a junction with the Pacific Crest Trail. Take trail No. 56 to camp at Dumbbell Lake, at 5 miles. The next camp is a scant 3 miles away on trail No. 1142 to Shellrock Lake. Next go 7 miles (long for children) on trails No. 1142, No. 1104, and No. 1105 to Blankenship Lakes. (From this camp you can take a 3½-mile day trip to Apple and Pear lakes.) The final stage is 3 miles, crossing Blankenship Meadows and heading back to Twin Sisters Lakes and the road. The loop covers a total distance, with side trips, of less than 30 miles and an elevation gain of about 2,500 feet. The map shows that shorter loops are possible.

If the loop is not practical, you can still explore lakes and ponds beyond counting. From Twin Lakes, Frying Pan Lake, surrounded by meadows, is a must. Other possibilities are Jug, Snow, Penoyer, Dumbbell, and Cramer lakes. Visiting them is like eating popcorn—once you start you can't stop. But each lake has a character all its own.

Mount Rainier National Park Highway

State Route 706

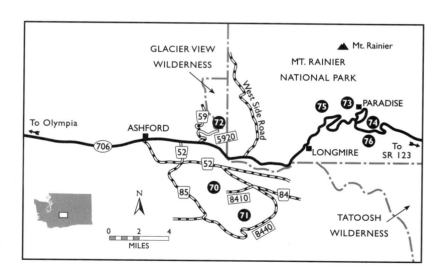

70. Bertha May and Granite Lakes

Type: Day hike or backpack
Difficulty: Moderate to difficult for children
Hikable: July–October
One way: ¼ mile, ¾ mile, and 1½ miles
High point: 4,175 feet
Elevation gain: 600 feet
Maps: Green Trails No. 301 Randle; U.S. Forest Service Gifford Pinchot
Information: Packwood Ranger District (360)494-0600

Three woodland lakes along a short forest trail are good choices for Scout groups or families with young and inexperienced hikers. Children can swim in all three, but shorelines are soft and muddy in the first two.

Drive Highway 706 east from Ashford 3.4 miles toward Mount Rainier. Turn right on Kernahan Road, signed "Big Creek Campground–Packwood," cross the Nisqually River, and in 1.5 miles turn left on road No. 52. Five miles from the highway go right on road No. 84. In 2 more miles, turn right on road No. 8410, signed "Teeley Creek Trail." Drive 3.9 miles to trail No. 251, elevation 3,600 feet. Watch carefully as the trail is poorly signed.

An easy ¼ mile leads to Pothole Lake, a poor name for a lake large enough for several campsites and for a sizable outlet stream.

Climb steeply ½ mile through big old hemlocks to Bertha May Lake. Long and narrow, her shore lined with driftwood and blueberries, Bertha May has good campsites. Too bad that many hikers visiting this lake are beginners who aren't used to carrying out their own garbage.

In ½ mile more, the trail

Mount Rainier from Bertha May Lake Trail

Sawtooth Range reflected in Granite Lake

climbs to the prettiest of the three, Granite Lake, elevation 4,175 feet. Good campsites are near the outlet and scattered around the far side. Near the outlet are picture-window views of Mount Rainier.

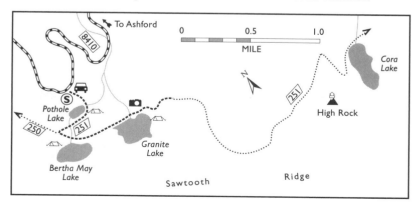

71. High Rock

Type: Day hike
Difficulty: Moderate for children
Hikable: July–October
One way: 1½ miles
High point: 5,685 feet
Elevation gain: 1,400 feet
Maps: Green Trails No. 301 Randle; U.S. Forest Service Gifford Pinchot
Information: Packwood Ranger District (360)494-0600

One of the few lookouts still operating in the state, High Rock offers children a rare opportunity to talk with the fire lookout operator and see the Osborne fire finder with which fires are located in minutes then called in on the radio. This tiny perch is no place for a sleepwalker. The spectacular views of Mount Rainier and tiny Cora Lake 2,000 feet below are like those from a small plane. Ask the lookout what it's like to be there in a storm—especially a lightning storm!

Drive Highway 706 east from Ashford 3.4 miles toward Mount Rainier. Turn right on Kernahan Road, signed "Big Creek Campground–Packwood." Cross the Nisqually River on a narrow bridge and, at 1.5 miles, reach a junction. Go straight ahead on road No. 85, circling the south side of the Sawtooth Range. Turn left on road No. 8440 and, at 11 miles total from the junction with road No. 52, reach the trailhead at Towhead Gap, elevation 4,301 feet.

Trail No. 266, signed "High Rock," begins on the uphill side of

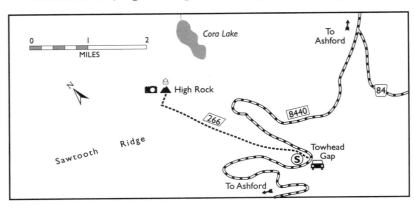

High Rock Lookout and Mount Rainier

the road and switchbacks steeply up through forest with occasional views of adjoining ridges. The last 200 yards are on steep solid rock into which handrails, painted for high visibility, have been set. At their end is the lookout, elevation 5,685 feet.

The building is perched on the corner of a precipice. In a burrow directly below it lives a family of marmots. They come out to bask in the sun on their airy ledge and ponder the view of Mount Rainier. In early summer, the young pups, much smaller than the adults, are extremely curious about hikers, especially the ones smaller than the adults.

72. Lake Christine

Type: Day hike or backpack
Difficulty: Easy for children
Hikable: July–October
One way: ¾ mile
High point: 4,802 feet
Elevation gain: 400 feet
Maps: Green Trails No. 269 Mount Rainier West;
U.S. Forest Service Gifford Pinchot
Information: Packwood Ranger District (360)494-0600
Wilderness permit required

A lovely little alpine lake in the Glacier View Wilderness offers campsites less than a mile from the road. The lake is shallow, but children will enjoy wading from logs and from the little peninsula on one shore.

Drive Highway 706 east from Ashford toward the Nisqually Entrance of Mount Rainier National Park. At 3.8 miles past Ashford, turn left on Copper Creek road No. 59. Drive 5 miles and then turn right on road No. 5920 and go another 2.4 miles to the trailhead, elevation 4,400 feet.

The first 100 feet of elevation gain on trail No. 249 are steep and badly eroded. Several portions of the trail have been sliced from a

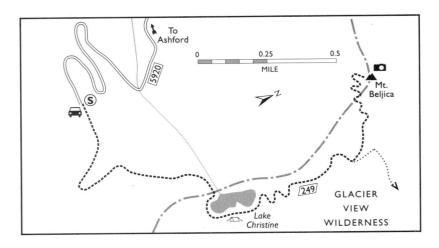

Mount Rainier from Mount Beljica

cliff; others are overhung by beetling cliffs. The ridges have been savagely clear-cut, and much of the remaining forest is by no means safe from the chainsaw since only the last ⅛ mile is protected wilderness. At ¾ mile is Lake Christine, elevation 4,802 feet.

Good camps, some with fireplace grills, are scattered on three sides of the lake. An interesting day trip is a 1-mile hike featuring a 700-foot ascent to the rounded rocky dome of Mount Beljica, elevation 5,475 feet. To do this, proceed along the same trail beyond the lake to a saddle and turn left on the Mount Beljica trail; a very steep ½ mile takes you to the summit. Enjoy the views of Mount Adams, the remains of Mount St. Helens, and the Puyallup Glacier of Mount Rainier. Notice the lookout building on far-off Gobblers Knob. Mount Beljica itself was once a lookout point but never had a building. Its unusual name is formed by the initials of the seven people who made the first ascent.

73. Alta Vista and Panorama Point

Type: Day hike
Difficulty: Moderate to difficult for children
Hikable: July–October
One way: ¾ mile and 1½ miles
High point: 6,900 feet
Elevation gain: 500 and 1,500 feet
Map: Mount Rainier National Park Backcountry Trip Planner
Information: Mount Rainier National Park (360)569-2211, ext. 3317

Take your pick. Walk a short but steep paved trail to Alta Vista overlooking Paradise Valley. Or continue on a steep rugged trail to Panorama Point and a magnificent view of Mount Rainier.

Drive to Paradise from either the Nisqually or Ohanepecosh entrances. Go past the Paradise Visitors Center to the large parking lot in front of the ranger station near Paradise Inn, 5,420 feet. Get there early; traffic is stopped at Nisqually when the parking lot is full.

A network of paved trails leaves from the Visitors Center. Climb the cement steps and follow the trail through the meadows. Children can look back at the Tatoosh Range from this perspective to compare it with later views. Pass the first trail for Alta Vista at about ½ mile; it is extremely steep. The meadows are a flower lover's paradise. The number of varieties of flowers that bloom here during the season runs into the hundreds.

In ¼ mile, find a better trail contouring west of Alta Vista and then dropping to a two-way junction. The Glacier Vista route is a

Marmot feeding in a Paradise flower field

Panorama Point and Tatoosh Range

bit longer but it's easier. Take the right-hand trail, climbing to a saddle overlooking Edith Creek Basin, and then go right again, climbing to the top of Alta Vista, elevation 5,940 feet, and the views overlooking Paradise Valley, the Tatoosh Range, and Mount Adams.

For Panorama Point, continue toward Mount Rainier as the

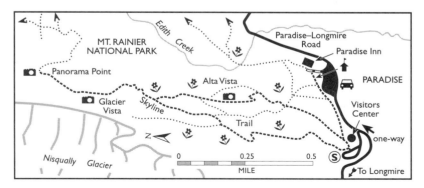

pavement ends. Along the ridge, watch for marmots and ptarmigans. In places, the trail climbs awkward stone steps where young children will need help. So will grandparents with creaky knees.

Last winter's snow patches are often encountered even in early August. At about ¾ mile, just below the switchback, is an ideal place to see the Nisqually Glacier. Scan it from its gleaming white snowfield near the summit down to the blue ice cliffs that often break off with a thundering bang. From here you can look into the crevasses and below to the rock-covered snout of the glacier. This is a good turnaround point if you can go no farther. But beyond the switchback, the trail is blasted from cliffs, with ever-increasing views. After a few more switchbacks it reaches Panorama Point, elevation 6,900 feet.

From the Point, you see over the top of all but the highest reaches of the Tatoosh Range to Mount Adams and Mount St. Helens. On a clear day, Mount Hood, 96 miles south in Oregon, can be seen. If kids sit quietly, they will hear the groans of massive Nisqually Glacier moving inexorably down the mountain. Have them watch for avalanches and for climbers moving up the snowfield toward Camp Muir on the most popular route. The immense rock tower on the skyline is Little Tahoma, and the block-shaped profile is Gibraltar Rock.

Paved Alta Vista Trail and Pinnacle Peak

74. Faraway Rock

Type: Day hike
Difficulty: Easy (but steep)
Hikable: July–October
One way: ¾ mile
Loop: 2½ miles
High point: 5,200 feet
Elevation gain: 350 feet
Map: Mount Rainier National Park Backcountry Trip Planner
Information: Mount Rainier National Park (360)569-2211, ext. 3317

This hike offers a magnificent view of the Tatoosh Range in one direction and Mount Rainier in the other. However, while children will be impressed standing on top of Faraway Rock, they will be even more impressed with the chances for wading in late summer ponds. Hang onto their hands; don't let them beat you there. A near vertical 200-foot cliff drops off on one side. The hike can be extended for a 2½ mile loop. The hike to Faraway Rock is on a portion of the eastern leg of the Lakes Trail, a 5½ mile loop from Paradise Inn to Reflection Lakes and back.

Artist's Pool and Tatoosh Range

Drive to Reflection Lakes from either the Nisqually or the Ohanepecosh entrance to Mount Rainier National Park (see Hike 76) and park near the eastern end of the larger Reflection Lake, elevation 4,860 feet.

Walk the road east past Little Reflection Lake and go left on the Wonderland Trail. In a couple hundred feet, the Wonderland Trail goes right. Stay left on the Lakes Trail. The way steepens. In a short ½ mile, cross a stream and continue climbing steeply to Faraway Rock, ¾ mile from the road, and stunning Artist's Pool with Mount Rainier reflected one way and the Tatoosh Range the other, elevation 5,200 feet. Photographers love this beauty spot, so you may meet tripod carriers seeking an undisturbed reflection who wish children would not make a ripple.

Look down on beautiful Louise Lake and across the highway to Bench Lake sitting on the edge of a cliff. Have kids guess by the telltale horn which of the Tatoosh Peaks is named Unicorn. The kids won't want to waste much time looking at the view, because the shallow lake will call to them to wade. If photographers are glaring, move up the trail several hundred feet to the beginning of High Lakes Trail and find two more pools where kids can join the frogs and polliwogs.

High Lakes Trail connects the east and west legs of the Lakes Trail. For the long way home, leave the ponds behind and walk the meadows on the side of Mazama Ridge. Mount Rainier is mostly out of sight, but views south to the Tatoosh Range are impressive. In a short mile, the way drops steeply to join the western leg of the Lakes Trail and then even more steeply for the ⅓ mile back to Reflection Lakes.

75. Comet Falls–Van Trump Park

Type: Day hike
Difficulty: Difficult for children
Hikable: Mid-July–October
One way: to Comet Falls, 2 miles
One way: to Van Trump Park, 3½ miles
High point: 4,900 feet
Elevation gain: 1,300 feet
Maps: Green Trails No. 269 Mount Rainier West; Mount Rainier National Park Backcountry Trip Planner
Information: Mount Rainier National Park (360)569-2211, ext. 3317

There are four good reasons to take this steep and rocky hike: (1) a spectacular waterfall, 320 frothing feet from brink to plunge basin; (2) alpine meadows; (3) Mount Rainier so close you can feel the glacier's cold breath; and (4) frequent glimpses of deer and mountain goats. The trail is steep with some big steps, and in many places it is also rough and rocky. Even so, this hike beside a noisy creek is delightful.

 From the Nisqually Entrance to Mount Rainier National Park, drive 10 miles toward Paradise to a small parking area signed "Van Trump Park" on the left side of the road, elevation 3,600 feet. (If you reach the bridge over Christine Falls, you have gone too far.)

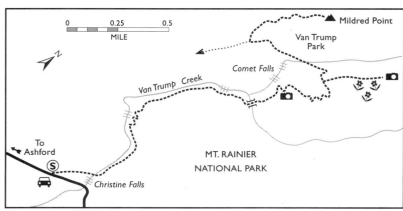

The trail starts up from the left side of the parking area and is wide and smooth as far as the bridge across Van Trump Creek. Stop on the bridge to look down into the rushing white water. Always within sound and often in sight of the creek, the trail climbs, sometimes steeply, over roots and boulders to the base of Comet Falls, at 2 miles, elevation 4,900 feet. Sitting in the spray and mist and gazing upward at the falling water can be so fascinating that children (and adults) lose track of time. A favorite pastime is to pick out a spot of water as it runs over the brink and follow it (with your eyes) until it blurs into the spray at the bottom.

It would be a shame to turn back here, so if you have enough energy, continue another steeply switchbacking mile (but on better trail) to Van Trump Park, where flower meadows extend into the very moraines of the Kautz Glacier, which tumbles from the summit ice cap. At 3 miles is a junction. Go right, climbing an exhausting staircase to a 5,700-foot viewpoint amid flowers and subalpine trees.

Comet Falls

76. Pinnacle Saddle

Type: Day hike
Difficulty: Moderate for children
Hikable: Mid-July–October
One way: 1½ miles
High point: 6,000 feet
Elevation gain: 1,200 feet
Maps: Green Trails No. 270 Mount Rainier East;
Mount Rainier National Park Backcountry
Trip Planner
Information: Mount Rainier National Park (360)569-2211,
ext. 3317

A breathtakingly lovely view across valleys to the southern majesty of Mount Rainier is reached by a short but steep walk above Reflection Lakes. Wide and safe enough for small children, the trail switchbacks upward 1,000 feet in 1¼ miles. Feast on the fat blueberries that line the trail in August and September.

 From the Nisqually Entrance to Mount Rainier National Park, drive toward Paradise. Pass Longmire and Christine falls, cross the Nisqually River, pass Narada Falls, and go right on the Stevens Canyon Road, signed "Ohanepecosh," to a parking area beside the first Reflection Lake. Stop to admire the mountain's reflection, a good reason for the lake's name. A quick search here for tadpoles is mandatory, but remember not to touch or disturb them. The Pinnacle Saddle trail starts on the opposite side of the road, elevation 4,854 feet.

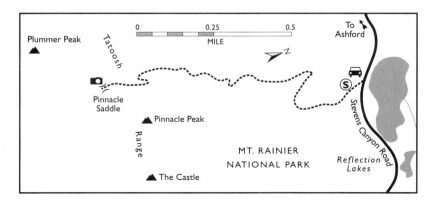

Mount Rainier from Pinnacle Saddle Trail

The smooth, well-maintained path crosses some snow patches, which in early summer may stop the trip short. Mount Rainier stays behind your back, so you may want to turn around for frequent rest-stop views. At the saddle, the trail is a shelf blasted out of Pinnacle's rocky shoulder. Hold children's hands here; the drop-off is abrupt. Turn around and gape. Above the lakes and Paradise are the moraines of Nisqually Glacier; follow the ice stream upward to the jutting buttress of Gibraltar Rock and, beyond that, the massive summit ice cap. At 1¼ miles and 6,000 feet, go through the saddle between Pinnacle and Plummer peaks for a whole new view of the South Cascades.

Climbers (and some in slippery shoes) often scramble up the hazardous cliffs to the top of Pinnacle Peak. This is not recommended for hikers and certainly not for children. Families will find plenty of satisfaction snacking amid the flowers.

White Pass Highway

U.S. 12

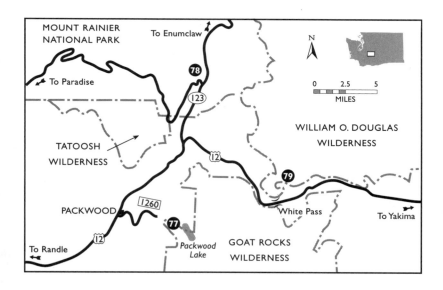

Grove of the Patriarchs

77. Packwood Lake

Type:	Day hike or backpack
Difficulty:	Moderate for children
Hikable:	June–November
One way:	4½ miles
High point:	2,857 feet
Elevation gain:	200 feet
Maps:	Green Trails No. 302 Packwood; U.S. Forest Service Gifford Pinchot
Information:	Packwood Ranger District (360)494-0600
	Wilderness permit required

One of the largest woodland lakes in the South Cascades is an easy stroll on a smooth, wide, and gentle trail. Camping, boating, and fishing continue undisturbed on a shore beloved by families since early in the century.

All is not well, however. The outlet stream was dammed in 1963 for a power project. Although the permit states that the lake level is to be maintained, it is often lowered. But, worst of all, the dam

Packwood Lake

was built 5 feet higher than it needed to be, so there is always the possibility that the power-hungry utility will flood the lakeshore. To add insult to injury, motorcycles, three-wheelers, and four-wheelers are allowed on the power company's service road to the lakeshore. But there they stop. The lake itself is off-limits to them.

Drive U.S. 12 south to the town of Packwood. At the upper end of town near the U.S. Forest Service ranger station, go right on the road signed "Packwood Lake." Enter the Gifford Pinchot Forest at 0.9 mile and drive 6.2 miles to a large parking lot and the start of trail No. 78, elevation 2,700 feet.

The trail starts in second-growth forest, entering the Goat Rocks Wilderness at ¾ mile. Watch for spectacular views of Mount Rainier. At 1½ miles, the old-growth forest begins. Children will be awed by these real-life giants, some at least 500 years old. Look, too, for groves of yew trees, whose bark is now being used in cancer treatment. Just before dropping to the lake, pass through an ancient rock slide that may have had a part in the creation of the lake by damming Lake Creek. At 4½ miles, reach Packwood Lake, elevation 2,857 feet.

At the lake are two guard stations, one of them a log structure built in 1910 and preserved as a historic landmark. A resort rents rowboats, rafts, and cabins in fishing season. A small store sells soup, sandwiches, and bait. The campground is just beyond the store. To escape the motorcyclists and their portable radios, lanterns, and beer, continue on to quieter campsites up the lake.

The partly glacier-fed lake, turquoise from suspended rock flour, has a large wooded island in the center. Above rises 7,487-foot Johnson Peak, where a band of mountain goats is headquartered. Originally named *Ackushnesh* by the Indians, the lake was renamed for Billy Packwood, who found it while prospecting with his son in the early 1900s. It was established as a Recreation Area in 1934 and then as a Limited Area in 1946, but that status was removed in 1962 so the dam could be built.

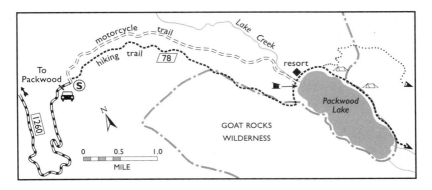

78. Grove of the Patriarchs

Type: Day hike
Difficulty: Easy for children
Hikable: May–November
One way: ¼ mile
High point: 2,200 feet
Elevation gain: None
Maps: Green Trails No. 270 Mount Rainier East;
Mount Rainier National Park Backcountry
Trip Planner
Information: Mount Rainier National Park (360)569-2211,
ext. 3317

The tremendous trees are bound to impress children—and grandparents too—with their size, age, and venerable beauty. There are interpretive signs for parents, hollow trees for imaginative children to crawl inside, and a shallow creek for everyone to soak or splash in. This is a great spot to cool off on a hot day, featuring a big wide trail to hike on a rainy one.

 Drive U.S. 12 south through Packwood and continue about 8 miles toward White Pass. Go left at the junction with Highway 123, signed "Mount Rainier National Park." Enter the park and drive past the campground to a major junction; go left on the Stevens Canyon Road,

signed "Paradise." Pass the entrance station and park on the far side of the Ohanepecosh River bridge. The trail starts beside the rest room.

The trail is mostly level. Look for the "squirrel overpass," a log suspended 10 feet over the trail like a freeway overpass. At a trail junction, turn right and descend a short switchback to a suspension bridge that spans a shallow branch of the river to a loop trail. Go either way, winding through

Hemlock root system in Grove of the Patriarchs

Nurse log in Grove of the Patriarchs

the Grove of the Patriarchs. There are thirty-five trees over 25 feet in diameter, some over 300 feet high, and all estimated to be between 800 and 1,000 years old. Notice that some of the hemlocks are standing in midair on giant roots. These trees were germinated and grown on nurse logs that long ago decayed and disappeared. Tell the children they provide homes for elves and other friendly woodland creatures.

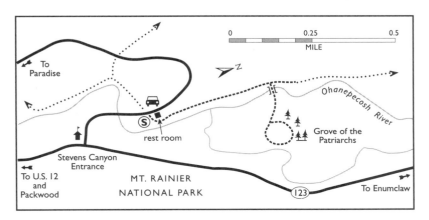

79. Deer Lake and Sand Lake

Type: Day hike or backpack
Difficulty: Easy for children
Hikable: July–October
One way: to Deer Lake, 2½ miles
One way: to Sand Lake, 3½ miles
High point: 5,295 feet
Elevation gain: 700 feet
Maps: Green Trails No. 303 White Pass; U.S. Forest Service Wenatchee
Information: Packwood Ranger District (360)494-0600
Wilderness permit required

These two neat and tidy lakes lie along the Pacific Crest Trail in the William O. Douglas Wilderness. Deer Lake is deep and surrounded by forest. Sand Lake, the farther one, is bordered by meadows and tall trees but is so shallow that, by midsummer, finding usable water can be a problem.

Drive U.S. 12 east to the summit of White Pass; 0.8 mile east of the pass is the Pacific Crest Trail crossing. Turn left and go 0.2 mile to the White Pass Campground and the hikers' parking area, elevation 4,400 feet.

Start out north in forest on the Pacific Crest Trail; in summer, this stretch is very dusty from horse traffic. At 1 mile, enter the William O. Douglas Wilderness. At 2½ miles, a short side trail leads to Deer Lake, elevation 6,206 feet, offering good campsites and a sandy swimming beach.

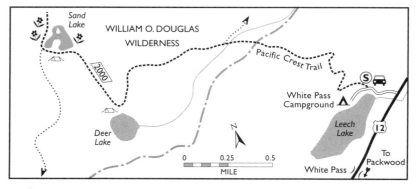

Another scant 1 mile brings hikers to Sand Lake, elevation 5,245 feet, and an interesting shoreline of alpine trees and flowers. A longtime hiker of these parts mused, after the most recent Mount St. Helens blast, "I always wondered where all this sand came from." (Mount St. Helens has been blowing "sand" for centuries.) Where the trail is cut into sidehills, exposing soil layers, you can see streaks of "sand" just like that now on the surface. Camping is just beyond the lake.

Pacific Crest Trail near Sand Lake

Sleeping Beauty Trail

South Cascades Highways

U.S. 12 and State Routes 503, 14, and 141

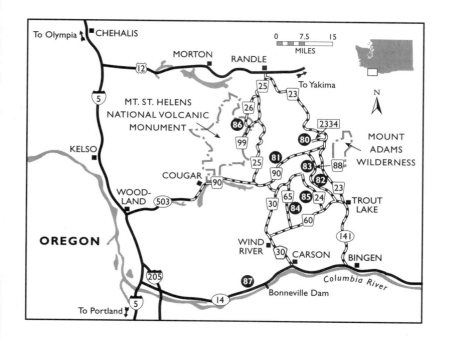

80. Council Bluff

Type: Day hike
Difficulty: Easy for children
Hikable: Mid-June–October
One way: ½ mile
High point: 5,180 feet
Elevation gain: 300 feet
Maps: Green Trails No. 334 Blue Lake; U.S. Forest Service Gifford Pinchot
Information: Randle Ranger District (360)497-1100

Plan this hike for a clear day. A very short climb through rock gardens leads to a spectacular viewpoint of Mounts Hood, Rainier, Adams, St. Helens—and Potato Hill too! If the Indians did not hold council meetings on this beauty spot, they should have.

Drive road No. 23 past Milepost 32, cross over Baby Shoe Pass (unsigned in 1996), and in about 33 miles go straight ahead on road No. 2334 for another mile to Council Lake Campground, elevation 4,221 feet.

A primitive road, barely usable by rugged cars or trucks, climbs 800 feet to the 5,000-foot level in 1.2 miles. If the decision is to drive, drivers will probably wish they had walked. However, hikers who find

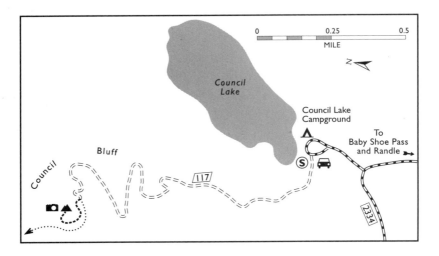

cars at the road end will probably wish they had driven. Take your pick. Either way leads to glorious views from an old lookout site.

The ½-mile walk to the 5,163-foot bluff carries hikers above surrounding ridges through clumps of flowers and juniper to knockout views of the Cascade volcanoes. Other landmarks in addition to those already mentioned are Steamboat Mountain, Sleeping Beauty, and Indian Heaven. Potato Hill? That is the cone with a small crater north of Mount Adams. In fact, everything you see here is either a volcano or lava flow.

Mount Adams from Council Bluff

81. Lewis River Trail

Type: Day hike or backpack
Difficulty: Easy for children
Hikable: Most of the year
One way: 2 miles
High point: 1,200 feet
Elevation gain: 200 feet
Maps: Green Trails No. 365 Lone Butte; U.S. Forest Service Gifford Pinchot
Information: Mount St. Helens National Volcanic Monument (360)2473900

The pride of the Gifford Pinchot National Forest is a gorgeous riverside walk among old-growth firs and cedars, past pools and rapids of the blue-green, glacier-fed Lewis River. Swimming, fishing, and camping are other good options. And the elevation is so low, the trail is open all year.

The Lewis River Trail can be reached either from Randle, by going south on road No. 25, or, as described here, from Woodland. Leave I-5 at Woodland, Exit 21, and drive north on Highway 503. Beyond the town of Cougar, the highway becomes road No. 90. Shortly after passing the upper end of the Swift Reservoir, turn right (still on road No. 90) and drive 5.2 miles. Turn left on road No. 9039, go 1 mile, and park next to the Lewis River bridge, elevation 1,000 feet.

Cross the bridge on foot and on the right find Lewis River trail No. 31. It begins in beautiful old-growth forest—fated to be just about the last preserved example of low-elevation big trees in this area. The way drops slightly and then levels to follow the river bank for ¾ mile. Nurse trees—downed logs sprouting new growth—give parents the chance to explain the birth-death-rebirth cycle of a forest left to nature's management. The trail moves from deep woods into second-growth deciduous trees and is bordered by oxalis, vanilla leaf, and heart-shape leafed vancouveria, named for Captain George Vancouver whose botanist, Archibald Menzies, found it in 1792. Briefly follow part of an old logging road; look for giant stumps from the *really* old growth, now gone. Visualize the logger of yesteryear balancing on narrow springboards inserted in the slots chopped in the sides. At about 1½ miles, is a high point where you can see the crystal-clear waters of Rush Creek gushing into the opaque green Lewis River. From here, the trail follows the river closely, passing moss-festooned maples and,

Lewis River near Bolt Camp

at 1¾ miles, a good campsite near a deep pool. Bolt Camp at 2 miles has a three-sided shelter built in the 1930s, still habitable and a lucky find in a rainstorm.

If time and energy permit, on returning to the car you can drive a scant 1 mile farther on road No. 9039 and walk the scant ½-mile trail to Curly Creek viewpoint. On the opposite side of the river, Curly Creek flows under a natural bridge and drops over a 60-foot waterfall directly into the Lewis River.

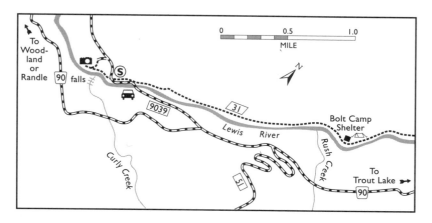

82. Sleeping Beauty

Type: Day hike
Difficulty: Moderate for children
Hikable: June–November
One way: 1½ miles
High point: 4,907 feet
Elevation gain: 1,400 feet
Maps: Green Trails No. 366 Mount Adams West;
U.S. Forest Service Gifford Pinchot
Information: Mount Adams Ranger District (509)395-3400

The rocky profile of a lady, best seen from the town of Trout Lake, provides hikers with a trail that ascends to exciting views of Mount Adams, Mount Hood, and the many little extinct volcanoes of Indian Heaven. Children love looking for the beauty stretched out against the skyline and then scrambling upward on switchbacks to the summit.

Sleeping Beauty can be reached by driving south from Randle on roads No. 23 and No. 8810 or, as described here, from Trout Lake. Drive west from the Mount Adams Ranger Station for 0.9 mile to road No. 88, turn right, and proceed north. At 5 miles, turn right on road No. (8810)040 and go 7 miles, passing a spur road, to the trailhead, elevation 3,500 feet.

Sleeping Beauty trail No. 37 begins on the south side of the peak. The way climbs steeply in an old forest of Douglas and grand firs. The wildflowers and undergrowth—buckbrush, pyrola, dogbane, wild rose, pipsissewa, and vancouveria—are typical of the dry side of the Cascades. The trail follows the base of the peak for about 1¼ miles to the north side, leaving the woods to emerge onto exposed rock. From

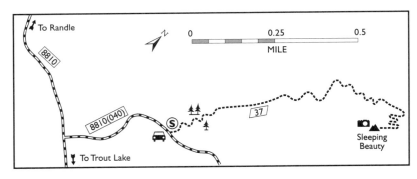

Sleeping Beauty

here, the trail switchbacks up ½ mile to the summit on tread blasted from the cliff. The steep side is banked up by a man-made rock wall; marvel at the hand labor it took to wedge tiny chips of stone vertically between larger rocks. At the summit, it is hard to tell whether the highest point is the beauty's nose or chin. Local residents get into arguments about this important issue. Whichever, the trail ends at 4,907 feet, on the lip of a cliff.

Old photographs show a lookout, built in 1931, surrounded by a sturdy fence. Both fence and building are gone now, so keep away from the cliff edge. In the lady's rock gardens, in season, find glowing lavender and scarlet penstemon, arnica, and valerian. Children will be exhilarated by the summit scramble and the feeling of being masters of all they survey.

83. Steamboat Mountain

Type: Day hike
Difficulty: Moderate for children
Hikable: June–October
One way: 1¼ miles
High point: 5,424 feet
Elevation gain: 800 feet
Maps: Green Trails No. 366 Mount Adams West;
U.S. Forest Service Gifford Pinchot
Information: Mount Adams Ranger District (509)395-3400

The stunning view of four volcanoes—Adams, St. Helens, Rainier, and Hood—makes clear why this was a lookout site from 1927 to 1971. Today, it is part of a Research Natural Area set aside for scientific studies by forest ecologists. Children can enjoy the spooky character of the old subalpine trees as the trail winds up to a summit cliff; once there, they can imagine being on the prow of a ship. Hang onto hands as you gaze down at three lakes and miles of forest and out to four massive ice mountains.

 Steamboat Mountain can be reached from Randle on road No. 23, from Trout Lake on road No. 88, or from Carson on the Columbia River by way of roads No. 81 and No. 24. The logging roads are such a maze in this part of the Gifford Pinchot National Forest that the traveler is well advised to obtain the Forest Service map, navigate to Mosquito Lakes near the junction of roads No. 24 and No. 8851,

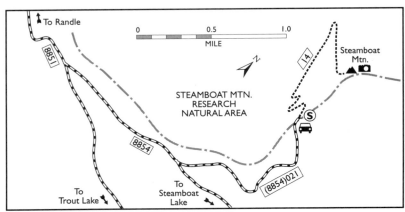

Mosquito Lake from cloud-shrouded Steamboat Mountain

and find road No. 8854, signed "Steamboat Lake." Drive 1 mile and go left, uphill, on road No. (8854)021 for another 1.4 miles to the road end and parking lot in a gravel quarry, elevation 4,700 feet.

Steamboat Mountain trail No. 14 is on the left side of the quarry. Before starting, look up at the awesome cliffs where the lookout once stood and where you will soon stand. Fortunately, the trail goes around the wooded backside.

The well-graded path is only a little over 1 mile long, but it's a very steep mile. Old subalpine firs with moss hanging from their branches create an especially spooky "guardian of the mountain" atmosphere. Just short of 1 mile, the trail reaches the crest of the ridge. Go right along the ridge to the summit, elevation 5,424 feet.

The east side of the broad summit is the edge of the cliff you saw from below. Look down to parked cars 800 feet below and out to spectacular views. We watched a raven that was level with us, only 50 feet away, riding an updraft. Keep a tight grip on small children here, lest they forget they don't have wings.

84. Thomas Lake

Type: Day hike or backpack
Difficulty: Easy for children
Hikable: July–October
One way: ¾ mile
High point: 4,300 feet
Elevation gain: 200 feet
Maps: Green Trails No. 365 Lone Butte and No. 166 Mount Adams West; U.S. Forest Service Gifford Pinchot
Information: Wind River Ranger District (509)427-3200
Wilderness permit required

Take a short, easy trail to a cluster of five lakes, the most accessible in the Indian Heaven Wilderness. It's a great place to swim and catch fish and offers any number of good campsites. (This would be an ideal hike to start a week-long vacation with small children, exploring the Indian Heaven Wilderness.) The trail is fine up to Thomas Lake, but

Thomas Lake

Centipede

beyond that, the horse riders, traveling while the ground is still soft from melting snow, have turned the tread into quagmire. Once turned to mud, the trail isn't passable again for hikers until after a month of dry weather.

By consulting the Forest Service map, you can find a way to reach the trail from Carson or Trout Lake. The directions here start in the town of Carson on Columbia River Highway 14. From Carson, drive north on the Wind River Road. Go right on road No. 65, signed "Panther Creek Campground," and drive some 17 miles to the Thomas Lake trailhead, elevation 4,100 feet.

Thomas Lake trail No. 111 starts out in a clear-cut dotted in season with Indian paintbrush and lighted by the white torches of beargrass. At ½ mile, the way enters the Indian Heaven Wilderness. At ¾ mile is a campsite between three lakes: Dee and Heather on the left and Thomas on the right. A few hundred feet beyond Thomas Lake is a junction; keep left to reach Eunice Lake. Lake Kwaddis is reached by a trail around Thomas Lake. All the lakes are at about 4,300 feet.

If you decide to explore the center of the Indian Heaven lakes country, head toward Eunice Lake and go right at the junction. The path gains 150 feet and then levels off and passes marshy meadows, shallow Brader Lake, and the quagmire left by horses. Children will be enchanted as forest becomes intermingled with parklike meadows dappled with ponds, pools, and lakelets.

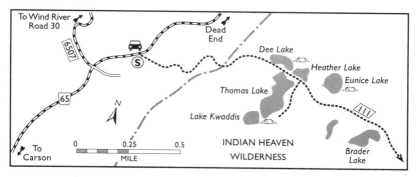

85. Indian Heaven Wilderness Vacation

Type: Day hike or backpack
Difficulty: Moderate for children
Hikable: July–October
One way: to Cultus Lake, 2 miles
Loop: 15 miles
High point: 5,300 feet
Elevation gain: 1,800 feet
Maps: Green Trails No. 365 Lone Butte; No. 366 Mount Adams West; U.S. Forest Service Gifford Pinchot
Information: Wind River Ranger District (509)427-3200 *Wilderness permit required*

Surrounded by a giant tree farm, Indian Heaven is a wild oasis, with 38 miles of trail through forest intermingled with parklike meadows, over 30 named lakes, and 100 or more nameless tarns. Indian Heaven

Bear Lake in Indian Heaven Wilderness

is one of the three best places in the state to take young children on a week-long backpack. There are nine trails leading into the long, narrow wilderness. The one recommended here is from Cultus Creek Campground.

Cultus Creek Campground can be reached from Randle on road No. 23, from Trout Lake on roads No. 88 and No. 24, or from Wind River as described here. Whichever route you choose, a Gifford Pinchot National Forest map is *essential* to figure out the maze of roads.

From Carson on the Columbia River, drive north on the Wind

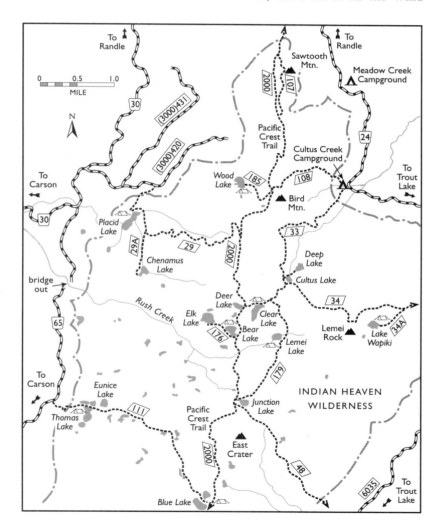

River Road to a junction near Milepost 30. Turn right on road No. 30, signed "Lone Butte," and drive to road No. 24. Go right, passing the Indian Berry Fields, to Cultus Creek Campground and park near the entrance, elevation 3,958 feet.

Trail No. 33 starts at the back of the campground and climbs steeply through forest (it gains 700 feet in the first mile) to a good view of Mount Adams. Thereafter, the trail is more moderate, climbing 400 feet in the second mile to Cultus Lake and campsites near the outlet, at 5,150 feet.

Bear Lake and avalanche lilies

Among the day trips from Cultus Lake is Deep Lake, a short distance away; the trail is near the outlet stream. For another side trip, continue on trail No. 33 for ¼ mile and then turn onto trail No. 34 and climb to a 5,600-foot viewpoint on the side of Lemei Rock.

The most fun is a lazy two- to four-way loop from Cultus Lake. Stay on trail No. 33, climbing over a 5,300-foot pass. In a scant mile, go left on trail No. 179 and camp near Lemei Lake, elevation 4,800 feet. Then move on for 1 mile to campsites at Junction Lake, elevation 4,700 feet, at the junction of trail No. 48 and the Pacific Crest Trail. From there take a 2½-mile side trip (each way) on the Pacific Crest Trail to Blue Lake. From Junction Lake you can also join the Pacific Crest Trail and hike north 1 mile to Bear Lake, at 4,700 feet. Camp here and, with the help of a map, find Elk, Deer, and Clear lakes. Then return to Cultus Creek Campground.

The entire loop can be hiked in a long day. But don't try. Take time to do all the important things—wading and swimming in the lakes and searching for tadpoles in ponds and frogs in the meadows. Because snow patches linger into August at this altitude, on a hot day snowball fights are inevitable. Just one precaution: All those lakes and ponds mean hordes of mosquitoes, so be prepared. But once in Indian Heaven, no child will ever want to leave.

Tadpoles

86. Norway Pass

Type: Day hike
Difficulty: Moderate for children
Hikable: Mid-June–October
One way: 2 miles
High point: 4,508 feet
Elevation gain: 900 feet
Maps: Green Trails No. 332 Spirit Lake; U.S. Forest Service Gifford Pinchot
Information: Mount St. Helens National Volcanic Monument (360)247-3900

A hot, dry trail through a desolation of timber downed by the 1980 blast of Mount St. Helens leads to one of the most spectacular viewpoints of the disaster area. You can look across Spirit Lake to the crater and smoldering dome. One-third of the lake is still covered by driftwood blown in by the eruption and washed into the lake in the ensuing tidal wave. On the lakeshore below Norway Pass, the giant wave swept everything bare for 500 feet up the hillside. Notice how the trees facing the mountain are lying flat in a straight line from the crater, while behind the ridge the trees are crisscrossed, an indication of how the turbulent wave of supersonic air eddied behind the ridge tops. Be sure to carry plenty of drinking water, which is available at the trailhead rest rooms; all shade trees have been flattened.

Drive road No. 25 south from Randle for 22 miles or drive 44 miles north from Cougar on roads No. 90 and No. 25 and turn uphill

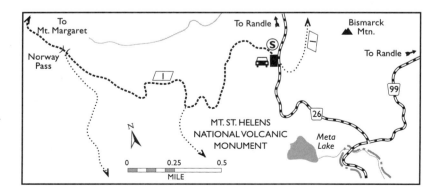

on road No. 99, signed "Mount St. Helens–Windy Ridge Viewpoint." At 8.9 miles from the junction, turn right on Ryan Lake road No. 26 and, in 1 mile, reach Norway Pass trailhead, elevation 3,600 feet.

The trail starts at the far end of the parking lot, first meandering a bit through fallen timber and silvery snags and then starting a long series of switchbacks above Meta Lake. At about 1¼ miles, the trail rounds a shoulder, drops a bit, and levels off. At 2 miles is Norway Pass, elevation 4,508 feet, and the view.

Everywhere new beginnings of life are springing up: fireweed, berries, and little firs. For some reason, the avalanche lilies on this hill flower with six or seven blossoms to a stem, unlike the usual pattern of two or three. The trail continues up Mount Margaret, but the views of the lake are no better higher up.

Log-covered Spirit Lake and Mount St. Helens

87. Beacon Rock

Type: Day hike
Difficulty: Easy for children
Hikable: Year-round
One way: Scant 1 mile
High point: 848 feet
Elevation gain: 600 feet
Maps: Green Trails No. 428 Bridal Veil, Oregon

The most famous rock in the Columbia Gorge makes a short and exciting hike for children, safe enough if they understand the hazards of stepping off the railed pathways. In 1915, Henry Biddle, Beacon Rock's original owner, began building the trail, some of which still bears the marks of his blasting. The rock was not set aside as a Washington State Park until Biddle, who had offered it to Washington and been refused, offered it to Oregon, which was eager to get it. At that point, Washington also became eager and accepted it. The views extend east to Bonneville Dam, west to Crown Point, and down to freight trains, boats, barges, and cars.

 From I-5 at Vancouver, drive east 34.5 miles on Highway 14, along the Columbia River, to the base of the towering rock and a large parking lot and rest room, elevation 250 feet.

The trail, wide enough to walk two abreast, begins on the west side of the parking lot. Circle the rock to the river side where the

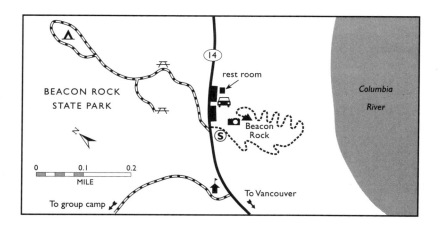

Beacon Rock Trail

switchbacks start up. Children are in no danger if they stay on the trail, but if the handrails are too high for short arms, parents may choose to hold children's hands instead. The way zigzags steeply upward. Wooden catwalks bridge cracks in the rock and, much to the children's delight, the trail itself, which lies a switchback below.

Views from the top are as exhilarating as those from the wing of an airplane. Gaze down on Bonneville Dam, across the river to Nesmith Point, northeast to Hamilton Mountain, and down at trains and ships below.

Olympic Peninsula Highway

U.S. 101

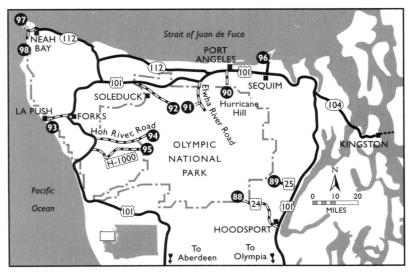

Campfire at Shi Shi Beach

88. Skokomish River

Type: Day hike
Difficulty: Easy for children
Hikable: May–November
Loop: 2 miles
High point: 1,000 feet
Elevation gain: 200 feet
Maps: Green Trails No. 167 Mount Steel; U.S. Forest Service Olympic National Forest/ Olympic National Park
Information: Hood Canal Ranger Station (360)877-5254

Walking this magical river loop in Olympic National Park can take as little as an hour. However, with small children, the possibilities for play along the way are infinite. Enormous trees with trunks set on stiltlike roots border river pools and rapids, calling to waders and paddlers. In fact, an hour is not enough. Better allow half a day.

Drive U.S. 101 along Hood Canal to Hoodsport. Turn uphill (west) on the Lake Cushman road, curving around Lake Cushman to the Staircase Ranger Station, elevation 785 feet. Look for a sign labeled "Staircase Rapids Trail" and another explaining that it goes along part of the route of the 1890 O'Neil Expedition.

Begin by crossing the North Fork Skokomish River on a gated bridge. Pass a park housing area and follow the level O'Neil Pass trail through deep forest by the Skokomish River. Pools and rapids are bordered by very old trees. Before this area became part of the park

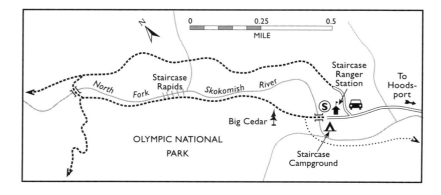

Bridge across the Skokomish River on Staircase Rapids Trail

there was some selective logging, but most of the remaining trees are at least 250 years old. Take time to admire the Big Cedar, ¼ mile to the left. It is 43 feet in circumference at the base. At the Red Reef, look for a deep pool beside a large red rock—a great place to swim. Beyond are a cedar with a root like an arm buried to the elbow, Dolly Pool, and the Staircase Rapids.

At ¾ mile, the trail divides. Go right past an enormous boulder overhanging the trail like half of a cave roof. Cross the river on an arched bridge, climb a few feet, and go right, completing the loop on an old road built in the 1930s. When the early summer flooding is over, there are many more pools and gravel bars to swim in and play on.

89. Lower Lena Lake

Type: Day hike or backpack
Difficulty: Moderate for children
Hikable: May–November
One way: 3 miles
High point: 1,800 feet
Elevation gain: 1,200 feet
Maps: Green Trails No. 168 The Brothers; U.S. Forest Service Olympic National Forest/ Olympic National Park
Information: Hood Canal Ranger Station (360)877-5254

Dominated by a shoulder of The Brothers, this forest lake was formed thousands of years ago by a massive rock slide that dammed the valley. The "dam" leaks and the lake resembles a reservoir in that the water rises and falls with the season. Wading and swimming are possible, but even in summer the water is so cold that only a child will enjoy it. This is one of the most popular hikes on the eastern slope of the Olympic Mountains, so the trail is eroded by the thousands of feet that have traveled it. Expect many roots and rocks for little feet to tumble over.

Lower Lena Lake has no protection. While Upper Lena Lake is in Olympic National Park and The Brothers is in The Brothers Wilderness, a hydroelectric proposal has Lower Lena Lake facing a possible road and logging.

Drive U.S. 101 along Hood Canal to a mile north of the Hamma

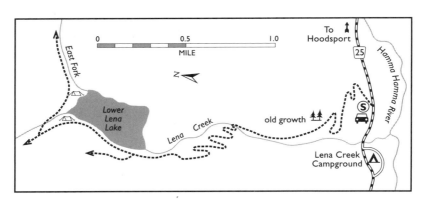

Lena Lake

Hamma River bridge. Go uphill on Hamma Hamma River road No. 25. At 9.5 miles from the highway, reach the Lena Lake trailhead, elevation 685 feet.

The trail switchbacks through an area that was first logged (by railroad) in 1931. The half-century-old trees look pretty good-sized until, at approximately ¾ mile, the trail enters old-growth forest, where you find the *really* big trees. At 1½ miles, the way crosses a dry streambed of Lena Creek, which runs underground most of the year. If time permits, explore the caves made by giant boulders lying on top of nature's dam and marvel at the size of the trees growing on it. That rock slide was a long time ago! At 3 miles, reach the shore and outlet of Lower Lena Lake, at 1,800 feet.

For camping, follow the trail around the lakeshore. When the lake is full, there will be a 150-foot climb over a rock buttress. At 3½ miles, at the inlet, are the best campsites, some of which have substantial fireplaces and even barbecue grills. Point out to children the scar on the hillside across the lake where the landslide came from.

90. Hurricane Hill

Type: Day hike
Difficulty: Easy for children
Hikable: Late July–October
One way: 1¼ miles
High point: 5,757 feet
Elevation gain: 700 feet
Maps: Green Trails No. 134 Mount Olympus; U.S. Forest Service Olympic National Forest/ Olympic National Park
Information: Olympic National Park Wilderness Information Center (360)452-0300

A stroll through flower fields on a gently graded asphalt path to the site of a former Forest Service lookout enables families to gaze at 360 degrees of glorious views. To the south lie the great chasm of the Elwha River and the peaks of the Central Olympics. Below is Port Angeles and the Strait of Juan de Fuca. Beyond the Strait is Vancouver Island. If the day is cloudless, look east for the San Juans and Mount Baker.

Hurricane Hill Trail

Hurricane Hill Visitors Center and supervisor

From Port Angeles, follow signs to the Hurricane Ridge road, pass the Olympic National Park Visitors Center, and enter the park. Pass the Hurricane Ridge Visitors Center at 18 miles and continue to the road end, elevation 5,000 feet.

Follow the asphalt path 1½ miles, gaining 700 feet, to the top of the hill. The meadows are dappled with clumps of subalpine fir and carpeted with lupine, valerian, penstemon, and paintbrush.

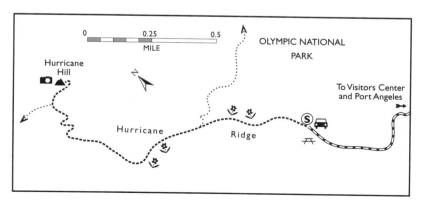

91. Olympic Hot Springs

Type: Day hike or backpack
Difficulty: Easy for children
Hikable: June–November
One way: 2½ miles
High point: 2,061 feet
Elevation gain: 300 feet
Maps: Green Trails No. 134 Mount Olympus; U.S. Forest Service Olympic National Forest/ Olympic National Park
Information: Olympic National Park Wilderness Information Center (360)452-0300
Backcountry permit required for camping

Soaking in small natural hot tubs set in Olympic National Park forest is a delight at any age, but families can enjoy the experience together at Olympic Hot Springs. A road walk of 2½ miles is the prerequisite; a large campground remains from the days when access by car was possible. Before that, in the 1920s, the area was a popular resort in an era when "taking the waters" at a hot mineral spring was an American passion. Families still make a weekend of it here, soaking by night or day.

 Drive U.S. 101 west from Port Angeles and turn left on the Elwha River road. Pass the Elwha Ranger Station (backpackers get overnight permits here) and then Lake Mills. Ten miles from the highway, reach the parking area, where the road is gated, elevation 1,750 feet.

The old road, shaded by tall trees, crosses a creek in the first ¼ mile. It is occasionally used by Park Service vehicles, but usually hikers

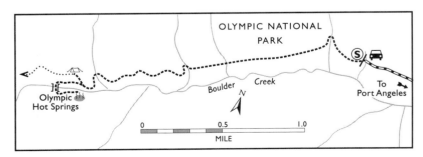

encounter only other hikers. Children can hold parents' hands and walk abreast. The mineral-scented steam drifting down the road reminds families of their destination, elevation 2,061 feet.

For camping, go right. For the hot springs, cross a bridge over Boulder Creek. The nearby signs reveal that the minerals present in the highest percentages are sodium and silica, which give the alkaline water a pH rating of 9.5. Children will be interested in the descriptive sign showing how surface water drops through rocks down to the earth's core, where it is superheated and then forced upward to form the hot springs.

Along the wooded path are at least seven pools to sample, ranging in temperature from lukewarm to 187 degrees! Most of the shallow, rock-lined pools are too small for more than two or three people. Two larger pools close together offer a family the opportunity to simmer in one and then cool off in the other. Take your choice of temperatures and degrees of seclusion. Depending on the other bathers, there may be some legitimate concern over water pollution; expect to encounter some skinny-dipping, too.

Olympic Hot Springs

92. Soleduck Falls–Deer Lake

Type: Day hike or backpack
Difficulty: Easy for children
Hikable: June–October
One way: to Soleduck Falls, 1 mile
One way: to Deer Lake, 4 miles
High point: 2,000 feet and 3,500 feet
Elevation gain: None to falls
1,500 to Deer Lake
Maps: Green Trails No. 133 Mount Tom; U.S.
Forest Service Olympic National Forest/
Olympic National Park
Information: Olympic National Park Wilderness Information Center (360)452-0300
Backcountry permit required for camping

This hike takes you through an old-growth forest with a green shag rug covering of moss and flowers to a thundering waterfall in a deep gorge. If the children are willing, climb to campsites near a subalpine lake.

Drive U.S. 101 west 2 miles from Lake Crescent and turn left on the Soleduck River road. Drive 14.2 miles, passing Sol Duc Hot Springs Resort, and continue to the road-end parking lot, elevation 2,000 feet.

With minor ups and downs, the broad smooth trail travels through a magnificent stand of old-growth fir, hemlock, and occasional Sitka spruce. In 1 mile, reach a junction and shelter with many campsites

and a good view of the falls from the trail bridge, elevation 2,000 feet. Children should be carefully supervised here, because below the falls is a deep canyon. **CAUTION**

To continue on to Deer Lake, cross the Soleduck River on the bridge, wet with the spray from Soleduck Falls. Children will enjoy standing here in the spray, watching the water drop. Beyond this point, the trail steepens in earnest. At 2 miles, you cross Canyon Creek and, at 4 miles, you reach Deer Lake and the campsites, elevation 3,500 feet. Spend a day here and wander up through heather and flower fields to High Divide, with its dramatic views across the Hoh Valley to the glaciers on Mount Olympus.

Soleduck Falls

93. Second Beach and Third Beach

Type: Day hike or backpack
Difficulty: Easy for children
Hikable: Year-round
One way: to Second Beach, ¾ mile
One way: to Third Beach, 1⅓ miles
High point: 300 feet
Elevation loss: 100 feet and 300 feet
Maps: Green Trails No. 163S La Push; U.S. Forest Service Olympic National Forest/Olympic National Park
Information: Olympic National Park Wilderness Information Center (360)452-0300
Backcountry permit required for camping

The most accessible of the truly "wilderness ocean" beaches of Olympic National Park's Pacific Ocean Section, prosaically named Second Beach and Third Beach, lie immediately south of First Beach, at the Quillayute village of La Push. They are wide and sandy at low tide, featuring spectacular offshore islands and sea stacks, surf, and beachside camping. Either beach can be a paradise on a warm day, but the same attractions can be enjoyed even in the long, gray months of winter.

Drive U.S. 101 to exactly 1 mile north of Forks and turn west on the La Push–Mora road. Drive 7.9 miles to a junction. Take the left fork toward La Push. (The right fork goes to Mora Campground and Rialto Beach.) At 3.9 miles from the junction is the Third

Sea stack from Second Beach

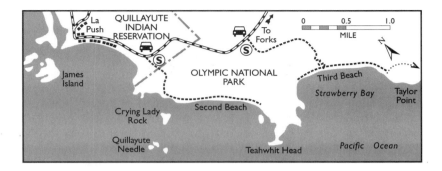

Beach trailhead, elevation 300 feet, and at 5.3 miles, only 0.8 mile short of La Push, is the Second Beach trailhead, elevation 100 feet.

The mostly level 1½-mile trail to Third Beach travels through old forest and then abruptly plunges off the plateau in a series of switchbacks before arriving at the long, curving beach of Strawberry Bay. Campsites in the creek ravine at the trail end are protected from the wind unless it comes from the west (which it usually does). On both

Driftwood stump

trails, getting across the wide belt of slippery driftwood onto open beach can be difficult and dangerous.

Walk the beach ½ mile south for a closer view of the waterfall plummeting down the sea cliffs of Taylor Point into the surf. Backpackers take the trail over Taylor Point to begin a 20-mile wilderness beach walk to the mouth of the Hoh River.

The ¾-mile trail to Second Beach is shorter, and the beach is wide and sandy and has more spectacular sea stacks and offshore islands. The last ¼ mile of the trail is down a wooden staircase to the shoreline. Campsites are very limited, but they can be found here and there on tiny benches above the high tide. (In the good weather of summer, during moderate tides, it is safe to camp on certain of the higher parts of both beaches.) Boil all water at both beaches.

Both beaches offer wonderful play possibilities: exploring tide pools, climbing giant driftwood logs, running in the surf. The temperature is the same winter and summer—bitingly cold. Whales are often observed from February to May, and throughout the year, eagles perch on snags. Bring a kite—there's always plenty of wind, and it drives the gulls crazy. Wear boots for walking around slippery rocks near the tide pools. Camping near the ocean can be memorable on a windless night—or a stormy one.

Third Beach

94. Hoh River Rain Forest

Type: Day hike or backpack
Difficulty: Easy for children
Hikable: Most of the year
One way: 3 miles
High point: 700 feet
Elevation gain: 120 feet
Maps: Green Trails No. 133 Mount Tom; U.S. Forest Service Olympic National Forest/ Olympic National Park
Information: Olympic National Park Wilderness Information Center (360)452-0300
Backcountry permit required for camping

The world-famous rain forest is accessible most of the year. Children will love seeing the huge Roosevelt elk, which through their browsing and grazing keep the forest floor cropped of undergrowth and looking parklike. The chances of seeing them are best in late fall and winter, when herds are down in the valley and most tourists are gone, but one resident band can be seen even in busy summer months. The Hoh River trail extends 17 miles, all the way to the edge of the Blue Glacier on Mount Olympus; however, families can amply savor the beauty of the rain forest in the 3 miles to the Mount Tom Creek trail junction.

 Drive Highway 101 north from Aberdeen or south from Forks and turn east on the Hoh River road. Drive 19 miles to the Hoh Visitors Center, elevation 578 feet.

Begin at the Visitors Center on a paved trail that turns to gravel and then soil. Hikers pass through old-growth Sitka spruce and Douglas fir interspersed with big leaf maple, all festooned with club moss and feathered with licorice fern. Elk have cropped the forest floor plants they find tasty, leaving a green carpet of ferns, moss, and oxalis. The most likely times and places to see the big animals, silently moving together, are early in the morning on the grassy terraces and gravel bars. One October morning when I was there, a large bull was moving his twenty cows across the terrace and through the river. A long strand of moss was draped rakishly across one horn. He bugled a challenge at me to make it clear they were *his* cows and I couldn't have them.

At 3 miles, reach the Mount Tom Creek trail and follow it to the

Hoh Rain Forest

bank of the Hoh River, elevation 700 feet. The river's grassy terrace offers excellent tent sites but build campfires on the gravel bar, not in the meadow. Children can play in the backwater pools.

Happy Four, at 6 miles from the Visitors Center, is an excellent destination for a second day. The old shelter there is highly appreciated during the rain spells, which provide the valley with 160 inches of rain a year.

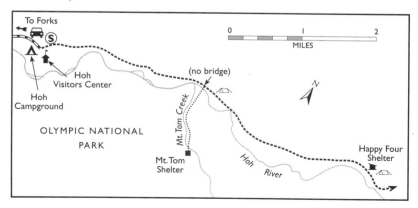

95. South Fork Hoh River

Type: Day hike or backpack
Difficulty: Moderate for children
Hikable: April–November
One way: 2½ miles
High point: 800 feet
Elevation gain: 120 feet,
Maps: Green Trails No. 133 Mount Tom; U.S. Forest Service Olympic National Forest/ Olympic National Park
Information: Olympic National Park Wilderness Information Center (360)452-0300
Backcountry permit required for camping

A gentle trail on river terraces leads into a uniquely beautiful old-growth rain forest. Children will be bemused to learn that the grazing of the elk maintains the open, parklike quality of this place; with luck, they may see some of the band. Another attraction is the chance for solitude—away from the crowds on the Hoh Rain Forest trail. While this trail has very little elevation gain, there are several ups and downs. About two-thirds is smooth and easygoing, but the remainder is rough, and toddlers will need help. For this reason the trail is classed as moderate.

Drive U.S. 101 from either Kalaloch or Forks to 0.6 mile south of the Hoh River bridge, near signpost 176. Turn south onto the Clearwater Corrections Center Road. At 6.7 miles, turn left and follow road No. H-1000, passing numerous side roads. (Watch carefully. Some may look like the main road.) At 7.4 miles, cross the South Fork Hoh River on a concrete bridge, pass the S. F. (South Fork) Hoh

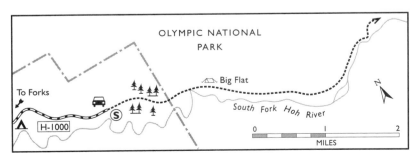

South Fork Hoh Rain Forest

Campground, and drive 2.8 miles more to the road end and trailhead, elevation 700 feet.

The trail begins by dropping briefly on rocky tread to a stand of young Sitka spruce. If the children clutch a handful of their bristly needles, they will see why elk prefer dining on young hemlocks instead. (Paradoxically, the favorite elk "salad" is devil's club, which should not make for a smooth swallow either!) At ¼ mile, enter Olympic National Park and, at ¾ mile, look for the first of the enormous old-growth firs on the right, or downhill, side of the trail. Its diameter is 9 feet, 8½ inches and its age at least 500 years. From here on, many 200- to 300-year-old firs, hemlocks, and spruces line the path as it travels up and down over six river terraces. The older, higher terraces have the oldest trees; alders, a "pioneering" species, cover the younger terraces made by the deposits of more recent floodways.

At about 1 mile, the trail drops to Big Flat, the first of the alder-grassy, open areas.

Between 2 and 2½ miles are fenced experimental areas from which browsing elk have been excluded since 1979. You'll have to search for them—they are some 50 yards off the trail. The startling contrast between the jungle inside and the open forest outside vividly tells of the enormous amounts of vine maple, salmonberry, currant, fern, and young trees the elk consume. The experimental areas at 2½ miles, immediately to the left of the trail, make magical picnic areas and resting places, with thick moss cushions, fallen logs, enormous old trees, and filtered sunlight playing on the wonderland beauty.

96. Dungeness Spit

Type: Day hike
Difficulty: Easy for children
Hikable: Year-round
One way: to beach, ½ mile
One way: to end of spit, 5 miles
High point: 100 feet
Elevation loss: 100 feet
Map: U.S. Forest Service Olympic National Forest/
Olympic National Park

One of the longest natural sandspits in the United States, Dungeness Spit thrusts out into the Strait of Juan de Fuca. A short descent through forest to the beach leads to its base. The spit is accessible to families at any time of the year; it also attracts harbor seals, killer whales, and bald eagles. The spit reaches far out in the strait and then curves inward like a gigantic arm, with a lighthouse in its "hand." Reaching the lighthouse requires a 5-mile walk, but there's plenty of fun along the way and no need to go more than 1 or 2 miles.

 Drive U.S. 101 to Sequim. In May and June, rhododendrons bloom alongside the highway. From Sequim, continue west a little over 2 miles on U.S. 101 to Kitchen-Dick Road, signed "Dungeness National

Harbor seals near Dungeness Lighthouse

Wildlife Refuge." Turn right and drive 3 miles to the road end, go right for 1 block on Lotzgesell Road, and go left on the Voice of America Road. Go 1 mile to the refuge and continue past the Clallam County campground to the spit parking lot. There is a $2 entrance fee.

The graveled trail wanders ½ mile through forest to a bluff above the Strait of Juan de Fuca and the first big view of the spit. Drop to the beach and begin the walk on the hard sand of the surf side. Tidal fluctuations will make a difference in the amount of beach exposed.

The beach is as pretty at the start as at the end. The views north are across the water to Vancouver Island, with Mount Baker floating above to the northeast, and southwest to the Olympic Mountains. Even a day in total

Driftwood and Olympic Mountains from Dungeness Spit

fog, with no view at all, is a mystical experience. Only the sound of foghorns will penetrate the velvet enveloping the spit.

To get away from crowds and for the best chances to see seals, marine birds, and migrating shorebirds, hike some distance. Killer whales, the famous orcas, are unpredictable visitors, but they often swim on the open side of the spit. Harbor seals supplement their fish diet with the eelgrass on the bay side. Older children may want to go the whole 5 miles and climb the steps of the lighthouse tower, built in 1857.

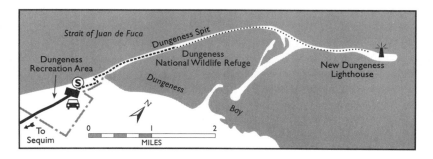

97. Cape Flattery

Type: Day hike
Difficulty: Easy
Hikable: Year-round
One way: ½ mile
High point: 300 feet
Elevation loss: 200 feet
Map: Green Trails No. 985 Cape Flattery

A newly constructed ½-mile trail leads to a platform overlooking the westernmost point of the contiguous United States, Cape Flattery, and Tatoosh Island with its red-towered lighthouse. Children will be

Cape Flattery cove

delighted by the chance to look down on whales and sea lions from the viewing platform. The trail descends gently on boardwalk, log rounds, and stone steps through dense forest, offering three other viewing platforms with different perspectives on the cliffs and coves. Along the way, rock portals below extend out on either side of the cape. The day I was there, a baby whale was spouting and swimming back and forth directly below the platform.

To drive to Neah Bay, take Highway 112 out of Port Angeles. Drive all the way through the town along the Neah Bay waterfront. At the end of town, turn left, following signs to Cape Trails, Fish Hatchery, and the Makah Tribal Center, an old Air Force base. At 6 miles past the sign, find the new trailhead and parking area. The trail was funded by the State Department of Transportation, the Department of Natural Resources, the Makah Nation, and the State Employment Security Department.

The sounds of the Tatoosh Island foghorn will call to children, who will want to run ahead. Because the trail is popular and crowded and the boardwalk is only wide enough for one at a time, they should not run. Tell them to walk slowly and to let the anticipation grow as they hear and glimpse the ocean from various windows. The rock coves and inlets have been carved and eroded over time by millions of waves. They represent the Juan de Fuca Plate and the North American Plate in collision at the edge of the continent. Children may not care about geology, but they will love searching for spouting, breaching whales and giant sea lions lounging on offshore rocks.

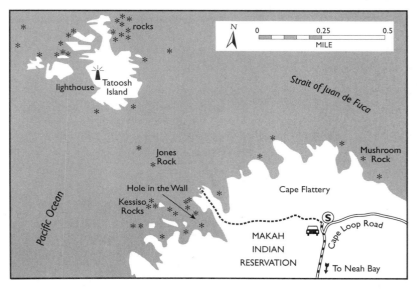

98. Shi Shi Beach

Type: Day hike or backpack
Difficulty: Moderate
Hikable: Year-round
One way: 2½ miles
High point: 50 feet
Elevation loss: 50 feet
Map: Green Trails No. 985 Cape Flattery

Children will enjoy a delightful secluded and scenic sandy ocean beach which curves out to the Point of Arches, offering wooded campsites during storms and high tides and beach camping for the fearless at Petroleum and Willoughby creeks. The access over Makah Nation land has been in question for years but is now available if one pays to park and avoid vandalism. Beachcombing along this beach is superb. Fishing net floats and all manner of flotsam and jetsam can be collected by children with sharp eyes. At low tide, there are tide pools and rock arches to explore. The hike out to the Point should not be attempted with small children or without a tide table.

 To drive to Neah Bay, take Highway 112 out of Port Angeles. Drive all the way through the town along the Neah Bay waterfront. At the end of town, turn left, following signs to Cape Trails, Fish Hatchery, and the Makah Tribal Center, an old Air Force base. At 2½ miles, go left on a dirt road and cross the Waatch River. Instead of turning right for Hobuck Beach, continue straight ahead, pass an old state park campground, cross the Sooes River, and wind around Anderson Point. Continue to a barricade across the road signed "Car Vandalism. No Parking." Unload packs, return to the closest house,

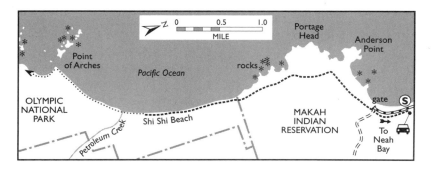

open the gate, park in the designated area, deposit a few dollars in an envelope in the box on the porch, and begin the ¼ mile walk back to the sign.

The old road was confiscated from the Makah Nation by the U.S. Coast Guard during World War II and never returned. The Makahs have since reclaimed it and denied access for a number of years. At the moment, they are allowing hikers to use the 2-mile road into the National Park, but they may retract the privilege again. This is a very muddy road and the children may have difficulty with deep mire. At points, there are bypass trails around the road, but some of the year it will be almost impassable. At the trailhead, drop steeply down the cliff on rock steps and switchbacks. A bull's-eye nailed to a tree trunk will help you remember the trail location on your return from the wide sandy beach. Walk as far along the beach as you wish but keep in mind that the tide may turn and cover your footprints and even come as high as the forest rimming the shore in some places. Beach fires are allowed.

Shi Shi Beach and Point of Arches

Deception Pass State Park

Whidbey Island Highway

State Route 20

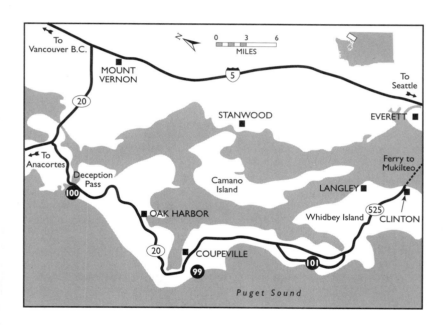

99. Ebey's Landing

Type: Day hike
Difficulty: Easy for children
Hikable: Year-round
Loop: 3½ miles
High point: 250 feet
Elevation loss: 250 feet
Map: None

In our family, the beach of the Ebey's Landing National Historic Preserve is the most beloved of the state's inland sea hikes. My children loved Ebey's Landing for its beauty, its history, and its endless opportunities for play. The trail on the bluff above the beach has some steep portions that are a struggle for toddlers. But once on top, my kids would gaze, entranced, down to the long tidal lagoon, west to Port Townsend and the Olympics, and south to Mount Rainier. Ebey's Landing Inn, listed on the National Historic Register, stands back in a field behind a locked gate. It is the old house with the distinctive moss-covered roof and tall chimneys. Colonel Isaac Ebey settled here in 1850 and was beheaded by Haida Indians in 1857. The inn, built in 1860, continued to operate until the 1920s. Its plans are on view in the Library of Congress, but it is not open to the public.

  Drive Highway 20 from either the north or south end of Whidbey Island. At 0.3 mile north of the Coupeville pedestrian overpass, by a power station, turn onto Terry Road, which becomes Ebey Road. At 1.75 miles from the highway, drop to a small parking lot at Ebey's Landing.

Those with very young children should walk the beach north 1 mile to Perego's Lagoon and devote the day to waves and driftwood. Families with older children can do a loop, starting either with beach or bluff. We always preferred to begin with the bluff. To do so, walk north from the parking lot and shortly ascend the low bank to a path paralleling the cultivated field. The bank tilts up steeply to become bluff, passing the front edge of a forest of Douglas fir, Sitka spruce, and pines contorted by prevailing winds. Trees lean picturesquely, framing Mount Rainier and the Olympics. The glorious views over table-flat Ebey's Prairie, right out of the nineteenth century (it's the most continuously farmed land in the state), include the Strait and the ocean horizon far beyond. Once atop the bluff, the level path is bordered by wild roses, broom, paintbrush, and wind-groomed salal.

Perego's Lagoon

At about 1½ miles, descend a steep trail to the north end of Perego's Lagoon below, where children can skip rocks and play in the drift-wood, watching for loons and seals in the waves. Walk south to your car along a shore offering superb beachcombing. Some years the lagoon has fresh water; in others the banks are breached and the lagoon is tidal. When this happens, the return trip is on a narrow path along the bluff side of the lagoon.

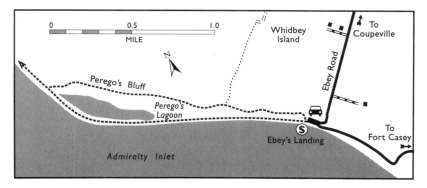

100. Deception Pass

Type: Day hike
Difficulty: Easy for children
Hikable: Year-round
First loop trip: 1 mile
Second loop trip: 2 miles
High point: 200 feet
Elevation gain: 200 feet
Map: None

Deception Pass is an ideal place to take children for a day, a weekend, or a week, offering lots of sand to shovel, scoop, and play in; a mammoth bridge to gaze up at; eagles to spot; boats to watch; and numerous forest trails to explore.

Leave I-5 north of Mount Vernon at Exit 230 and drive Highway 20 west to Fidalgo Island. On the island, follow signs to Deception Pass. Enter Deception Pass State Park at Pass Lake and drive on the Deception Pass Bridge. If you wish, stop on Pass Island to walk out on the bridge and watch the boats below fighting against or going with

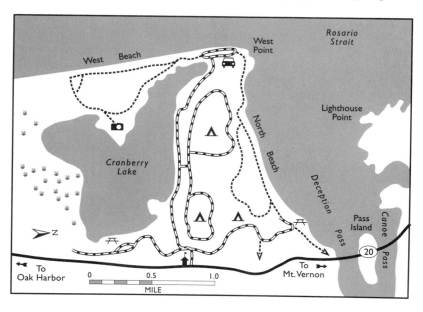

the strong currents. Then continue on to Whidbey Island and go right into the Deception Pass Park headquarters area to the large parking lot at West Beach.

There are many trails to explore, but the two described here are my favorites with children. If your children are like mine, they will first head for the sand dunes. On the Cranberry Lake side of the parking lot, find the paved trail behind the rest rooms. The trail passes a series of dunes covered with sedge, beach morning glory, and beach pea. A sign marked "Foredunes" describes those closest to the shoreline. Stay on the trail. The vegetation and dunes are too fragile even for little feet. In ¼ mile, reach the park boundary. For sand play, turn right and go to the beach. For a 1-mile loop hike, go left past more sand dunes signed "Precipitation Dunes."

Totem at West Beach

Climb a wooden platform for an overlook of marshes and tea-colored Cranberry Lake. Yes, wild cranberries grow here—some at the edge of the lake. Another bog plant, Labrador tea, also thrives in this acid soil. (You can recognize it by its small, leathery yellow-green leaves.) Rub a leaf and hold it next to your face to smell its pungent aroma.

The 2-mile second loop hike begins at the other end of the parking lot and takes the trail over the rocky headland of West Point and then drops to the first beach of North Bay. Expect to see large old Douglas firs framing views of the water, which will probably be filled with sailboats, fishing vessels, and tugboats pulling logs, all waiting until the tide turns and runs in their direction. From the first bay, bear left into woods past a car campground and go about ¼ mile to the next beach. At low tide, the beach can be walked. Look up at the bridge and note how small the people standing on it seem. Look still higher for eagles soaring (we saw four one March day) above the water. You can also see scaups, coots, scoters, and all kinds of ducks. Continue ¼ mile to the third beach. At the headland above the third beach, turn right and follow the curving road up past park headquarters and then downhill past Cranberry Lake to the parking lot.

101. Classic U or Wilbert Trail

Type: Day hike
Difficulty: Easy for children
Hikable: Year-round
Loop: 2 miles
High point: Sea level
Elevation gain: None
Map: None

A large stand of old-growth trees within South Whidbey State Park is the last vestige of ancient forest on the island. Giant Douglas firs, Sitka spruce, and cedars blend with younger hemlocks and deep forest undergrowth, perhaps grown up since a long-ago forest fire swept through the stand. Children can actually climb inside some of the old trees. Though the trees are still living, their trunks have ground-level hollows that call out to be explored. Wilbert is the name of one of the Whidbey residents who fought to save the old growth from being cut. The 225-acre forest area is also called *Classic U* because it was once owned by the University of Washington. The loop trail is mostly level and can be walked at all times of the year and in any weather. Despite the fact that the park is closed in winter, the trail can be hiked at any time.

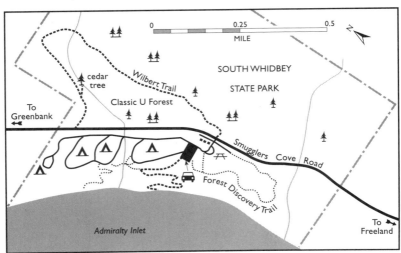

Ancient Cedar on the Wilbert Trail

From the Clinton ferry terminal, drive past Freeland and, at about
10 miles, go left on the Bush Point Road signed "South Whidbey State
Park." At 3.6 miles, the Bush Point Road goes left. Continue straight
ahead on what becomes Smugglers Cove Road leading to South Whidbey
State Park. Park in the parking lot on the west side of the road and
find the Wilbert trailhead on the east side.

The jewel of the park and the place where kids will head first
is the beach, some 250 feet below the day-use area at the second
parking area. A short ½-mile beach trail starts from there.

Not so popular, but also a jewel, are the big trees along the Wilbert
Trail. Begin among ferns and old firs and listen for the sounds of
woodpeckers. Cross an old utility road and find horizontal rotting

Beach trail at South Whidbey State Park

cedar logs next to ancient cedar trees. Some of them have spooky shapes and scorched and charred places on their bark, like scars from the long-ago fire. The sounds of the highway dwindle and the songs of birds increase. A number of steps have been cut in places which might be muddy, and trail maintenance crews have taken out some trees felled by wind. In winter, spaghnum moss on tree trunks turns bright green and pockets of ferns show up in the crotches of trees. At 1¼ miles, find a sign for the Ancient Cedar. Children should examine this wonderful old tree closely. Its base is dissected by decay, allowing little ones to crawl inside. Cross the highway to find the trail continuation and group campsite. For the loop, walk the campground road back ¾ mile to the starting point.

Index

About the Author

Seattle resident Joan Burton was herself introduced to hiking as a child, and by the time she had reached her teens, she had climbed the six highest mountains in Washington. Later, as a parent with growing children, she was involved in introducing not only her own family to the joys of outdooring but also members of the Girl Scout and Cub Scout groups of which she was leader. Burton is a long-time member of The Mountaineers and a graduate of both the basic and intermediate climbing courses taught by that club. After a number of years teaching high school English, Burton is now a program assistant to the University of Washington Retirement Center. She has published several magazine articles on outdoor subjects; this is her first book.

THE MOUNTAINEERS, founded in 1906, is a nonprofit outdoor activity and conservation club, whose mission is "to explore, study, preserve, and enjoy the natural beauty of the outdoors. . . . " Based in Seattle, Washington, the club is now the third-largest such organization in the United States, with 15,000 members and five branches throughout Washington State.

The Mountaineers sponsors both classes and year-round outdoor activities in the Pacific Northwest, which include hiking, mountain climbing, ski-touring, snowshoeing, bicycling, camping, kayaking and canoeing, nature study, sailing, and adventure travel. The club's conservation division supports environmental causes through educational activities, sponsoring legislation, and presenting informational programs. All club activities are led by skilled, experienced volunteers, who are dedicated to promoting safe and responsible enjoyment and preservation of the outdoors.

If you would like to participate in these organized outdoor activities or the club's programs, consider a membership in The Mountaineers. For information and an application, write or call The Mountaineers, Club Headquarters, 300 Third Avenue West, Seattle, Washington 98119; (206) 284-6310.

The Mountaineers Books, an active, nonprofit publishing program of the club, produces guidebooks, instructional texts, historical works, natural history guides, and works on environmental conservation. All books produced by The Mountaineers are aimed at fulfilling the club's mission.

Send or call for our catalog of more than 300 outdoor titles:

The Mountaineers Books
1001 SW Klickitat Way, Suite 201
Seattle, WA 98134
1-800-553-4453
e-mail: mbooks@mountaineers.org
website: www.mountaineers.org

Other titles you may enjoy from The Mountaineers:

BEST HIKES WITH CHILDREN® IN WESTERN WASHINGTON & THE CASCADES, Volume 2, *Joan Burton*
A guide to day hikes and overnighters for families, with tips on hiking with kids, safety, and fostering a wilderness ethic. Includes points of interest, trail descriptions, information on flora and fauna, campsite locations, and maps.

AN OUTDOOR FAMILY GUIDE TO WASHINGTON'S NATIONAL PARKS: Mount Rainier, Mount St. Helens, North Cascades, The Olympics,
Vicky Spring & Tom Kirkendall
A three-season guide to the best selection of outdoor activities in Washington's spectacular national parks, including four major tourist destinations in scenic Washington.

KIDS IN THE WILD: A Family Guide to Outdoor Recreation,
Cindy Ross & Todd Gladfelter
A family-tested handbook of advice on sharing outdoor adventures with children of all ages and skill levels, with recommendations on equipment, food, safety, and family activities.

EXPLORING WASHINGTON'S WILD OLYMPIC COAST,
David Hooper
The most detailed guide available to hiking the beaches of Olympic National Park, with advice on camping, safety, wildlife, human history, and shipwrecks.

MAC'S FIELD GUIDES: Northwest Park/Backyard Birds, Northwest Trees, Pacific Northwest Wildflowers,
Craig MacGowan & Sauskojus
Two-sided plastic laminated cards developed by a teacher of marine science, with color drawings, common and scientific names, and information on size and habitat.

ANIMAL TRACKS: PACIFIC NORTHWEST, Book & Poster,
Chris Stall
Both book and poster offer information on 40–50 animals common to the Pacific Northwest region.

WASHINGTON STATE PARKS: A Complete Recreation Guide,
Marge & Ted Mueller
One of the series of multi-season, multi-activity regional guides, with maps, directions and information on park facilities.

Outdoor Books by the Experts

Whatever the season, whatever your sport, The Mountaineers Books has the resources for you. Our FREE CATALOG includes over 350 titles on climbing, hiking, mountain biking, paddling, backcountry skiing, snowshoeing, adventure travel, natural history, mountaineering history, and conservation, plus dozens of how-to books to sharpen your outdoor skills.

All of our titles can be found at or ordered through your local bookstore or outdoor store. Just mail in this card or call us at 1·800·553·4453 for your free catalog.

Name _____
Address _____
City _____ State _____ Zip+4 _____-_____
E-mail _____

Please send another catalog to my friend at:
Name _____
Address _____
City _____ State _____ Zip+4 _____-_____
E-mail _____

564-6

Attention Western Washington residents:

Wanna go outside and play?

Join The Mountaineers today!

You may think we're just a climbing club but The Mountaineers offer a lot more. We sponsor regular outings and classes on hiking, backcountry skiing, backpacking, alpine scrambling, bicycling, first aid, photography, sailing, sea kayaking, trail maintenance, and conservation. There are activities for families, singles, and active people of all ages. Other benefits of joining The Mountaineers include the use of four terrific mountain lodges and the opportunity to join our exotic foreign excursions. And, of course, we offer hundreds of climbs each year for all levels of experience.

If you live in Western Washington, there's a Mountaineers Club near you. To receive membership information, just mail in this card today!

300 Third Avenue West
Seattle, WA 98119
206·284·6310
www.mountaineers.org

Name _____
Address _____
City _____ State _____ Zip+4 _____-_____
E-mail _____

564-6

NO POSTAGE
NECESSARY
IF MAILED
IN THE
UNITED STATES

BUSINESS REPLY MAIL

FIRST-CLASS MAIL   PERMIT NO. 85063   SEATTLE, WA

POSTAGE WILL BE PAID BY ADDRESSEE

THE MOUNTAINEERS BOOKS
1001 SW KLICKITAT WAY STE 201
SEATTLE WA 98134-9937

NO POSTAGE
NECESSARY
IF MAILED
IN THE
UNITED STATES

BUSINESS REPLY MAIL

FIRST-CLASS MAIL   PERMIT NO. 75491   SEATTLE, WA

POSTAGE WILL BE PAID BY ADDRESSEE

THE MOUNTAINEERS
300 3rd AVE W
SEATTLE WA 98119-9914